We find it very reassuring to discover, that the very things from our collection which appeal most in one country appeal equally from Tulsa to Tokyo. It gives us a marvellous feeling, as if the world starts to beat with one heart.

This is not to say that there is a dominant style being bought: varied prints reproduced from epochs with centuries between them are equal favourites. Perhaps it's the historical connection itself that appeals, as we all respond to the lovely endless march of nature and what we can create from it.

Such enthusiasm makes us bolder. There is more spice this year with our traditional sweetness: a complete gentleman's apartment to underline the fact, and civilised Chinoiserie for the sober. In fact, there was such a crush of ideas for 1986 that what you see in this book are only the very best of them.

Nick Ashley.

DECORATING WITH LAURA ASHLEY

IDEAS TO INSPIRE

Decorating a house should be a wonderful opportunity to indulge your ideas on interior design, but can all too easily become a nightmare in which everything looks out of place. Whether or not naturally talented, we are all capable of achieving success. The great secret is to take advice, adjusting a provenly effective decorative scheme to suit your own personal taste.

In the first part of this magazine you will find a selection of interiors carefully chosen to show Laura Ashley's creative response to a number of totally different decorating problems, presented to us by a variety of people. These range from the spacious grandeur of neo-classicism to an endearingly modest scale of rural simplicity.

While you might not choose to exactly recreate any one of these complete design concepts in your own home (although it may suit you to do just that), we think that they demonstrate what it is possible to achieve with a little careful planning. And they will, we hope, provide all the inspiration you need to transform any room, perfectly.

CONTENTS

Gentleman's Apartment, Antwerp
Drawing Room _____ 4
Bedroom _____ 8
Bathroom _____ 12
Kitchen _____ 16

Town House, Florida
Dining Room _____ 18
Drawing Room _____ 22
Hall _____ 26
Verandah _____ 28
Bedroom _____ 32

Farmhouse, Northern England
Bathroom _____ 34

Period Cottage,
Home Counties, England
Kitchen _____ 36

Farmhouse, Mid-Wales
Scullery _____ 38
Bedroom _____ 40

Château, Picardy, Northern France
Conservatory _____ 44

Country House,
West Country, England
Bathroom _____ 48

FURNISHING PRODUCTS

THE ELEMENTS OF STYLE

'Of course, it all looks marvellous when it's finished, but I could never hope to achieve anything like that.'

Take another look. All of the room-sets illustrated in the first section of this magazine — bedrooms, drawing rooms, bathrooms, kitchens and dining rooms — have been created using Laura Ashley furnishing products.

In the second section the products are taken out of their domestic settings, allowing you to see quite

CONTENTS

Introduction _____ 50
Wall Coverings _____ 52
Fabrics
Country Furnishing Cotton ___ 56
Lining Fabric _____ 61
Drawing Room Fabric _____ 62
Linen Union _____ 66
Upholstery Fabric _____ 68
Dobby _____ 69
Chintz _____ 70
Plastic Coated Fabric _____ 74
Borders _____ 75
Wallpaper Borders, Fabric Borders.
Trimmings _____ 80
Bias Binding, Braid, Fringing, Gimp, Tie-backs.
Paint _____ 82
Tiles _____ 84
Lighting _____ 88

clearly just what is available in each particular range before you make your choice as to what is suitable for your individual taste and needs.

Within these pages you will find everything from wallpaper to lamp-shades, from chintz to tiles and braid. In fact, all those essential elements needed to convert the basic framework of any decorative scheme into a room of charm and character.

PRINTS & COLOURWAYS

GUIDE TO CO-ORDINATION

How can one furnish a room using blocks of colour and a number of different prints, on curtains, walls and furniture, and still be certain that no two shades will clash and no two patterns act against each other to produce a discordant mess?

Laura Ashley's answer is straightforward co-ordination.

In this third section of the catalogue you will find details of all the designs and colours featured in the collection laid out in a simple

and easy-to-use system of colour groupings. At a glance you can see just how your own choice of colours and designs will work together to complement each other in the room as a whole. At the same time a series of symbols tells you instantly what products are available in each particular print and colourway.

Now, with the help of Laura Ashley, you can begin to discover just how simple and enjoyable an exercise it is to plan and execute successful interior decoration.

CONTENTS

Dining Collection _____ 92
Tablecloths, Place-mats, Cosies, Napkins, Apron, Oven Gloves, Trays.

Crafts _____ 95
Tapestry Cushions, Patchwork Pieces.

Cushions _____ 96
Patchwork Quilts _____ 98
Lace _____ 100
Tea for Two Set _____ 100
Bedlinen _____ 102
Dressing Room Collection ___ 108
Desk Collection _____ 109
Towels _____ 110
Made to Measure Services ___ 111
Curtains, Blinds, Pelmets, Tie-backs.

Upholstered Furniture _____ 116
Interior Design Service _____ 120

Introduction _____ 122
Crimson, Buttermilk & Jade __ 124
Kingfisher & Smoke _____ 128
Sand, Navy & Burgundy _____ 132
Sand, Navy, Burgundy
& Dark Green _____ 136
Sage & Plum _____ 142
Sapphire & Mustard _____ 146
Poppy & Black _____ 152
Denim & Tropical Green ____ 154

Terracotta & Moss _____ 156
Rose _____ 160
Aquamarine & Apricot _____ 166

Customer Information _____ 170

U.S.A. Shop Addresses _____ 174

Laura Ashley Publications ___ 175

AN ENGLISHMAN ABROAD
DRAWING ROOM
GENTLEMAN'S APARTMENT
ANTWERP BELGIUM

In spacious city apartments, in country homes or in sleek modern town houses, English style is at home all over the world and this bachelor apartment in Antwerp proves the point by demonstrating the style at its most inventive.

Quiet sage green is mixed with warmer sand colours and smoke blue in a selection of differing fabric designs and paint. These blend effortlessly together to give a timeless quality and an effect that is both sophisticated yet thoroughly comfortable – ideal in this town house apartment.

Rooms like this one, with its grand proportions, invite grand treatment and lavish use of fabric. Large windows demand well-proportioned curtains and the draped pelmets are inspired by early nineteenth century Empire designs.

We are sticklers for detail. We feel it is the smaller touches like the colour of pipings on the cushions, and the thick cotton bullion fringes and tassels, dyed to match the fabric colours, that link the various elements of the room together.

While Laura Ashley is known the world over for her pretty country cottons and sprig designs, we have found a new side to our talents by creating fabrics with a masculine look, making a room that is essentially English yet at home in a cosmopolitan city.

Patterns of the past are a strong inspiration for present day living. It is in rooms like this elegant drawing room that fabrics with a timeless quality to their design work extra well. The curtain fabric (picture 1 overleaf) is Laura Ashley's recently-introduced Grapes design in smoke and sage colours. It is adapted from a design for a seventeenth century table carpet. Made in practical linen union, the design imitates needlework. The heavy cotton

1▲

2▲

3▲

4▲

5▼

6▲

7▼

bullion fringe is dyed to match the new smoke colours and adds to the Empire feeling of the curtains with their draped pelmet.

Taking the curtain colours as the basis, we selected a group of small accessory prints for the chairs and the ottoman. The comfortable armchair (picture 2) is upholstered in Laura Ashley blue Paisley. Edges are piped in plain sage. The ottoman (picture 3) with its antique paw feet is upholstered in another accessory print. Thick bullion fringe was sewn round the cushion base to break up the sharp box shape and add to the Edwardian club-like effect.

On the buttoned chair (picture 4) is the classic background print, Nutmeg. This has a Victorian feel that goes well with the age of the chair. The cushion matches the curtains, but this time the needlework is real, made from one of Laura Ashley's special tapestry sewing kits in the Grapes design.

While an antique throwover shawl would be expensive to buy for a sofa, a much less costly alternative is this large square of linen (picture 5). The fabric is Laura Ashley's green Florentina, a useful flamestitch pattern with an antique feel to it. The cloth is edged in cord, its corners decorated with tassels. The sofa back (picture 6), which would otherwise be a solid block of green, is made to look much more interesting with the casually arranged tasselled drape. Lampshades are made from our country furnishing cotton in cream. In the corner of the room (picture 7) an antique marble bust found in the Paris flea market presides above the comfortable chair, with its collection of contrasting cushions, all in Laura Ashley fabrics. The plain green one is decorated with one of our fabric borders in smoke.

Elaborate panelling (picture 8) was treated traditionally in two colours with Laura Ashley's sage and sand paints. We chose the sage green, because we wanted a colour that was peaceful and not too dark. Picking out the architectural detail in sand colour was a good way of emphasising the contours of the old panelling and tying in the main colours of the room.

On the desk (picture 9) are a series of bound books, patterned frames and other accessories from the Laura Ashley Desk Collection, chosen for their co-ordinating smoke blue.

Curtains in Linen Union, Grapes, Smoke Multi Cream.	
Armchair in Upholstery Fabric, Paisley, Smoke/Kingfisher/Cream, piped in plain Sage.	
Buttoned Chair in Country Furn. Cotton, Nutmeg, Cream/Sage with cushion made from tapestry sewing kit, Grapes, Smoke Multi Cream.	
Throwover Shawl in Linen Union, Florentina, Dark Green Multi Stone.	
Lampshades made in plain Country Furnishing Cotton, Cream.	
Square Cushions made in plain Country Furnishing Cotton, Sage with **Appliquéd Fabric Border**, Trompe, Kingfisher/Stone.	
Round Frilled Cushion Paisley, Smoke/Kingfisher/Cream.	
Panelled Walls in Light Sage and Sand Flat Paints.	

AN ENGLISHMAN ABROAD
BEDROOM
GENTLEMAN'S APARTMENT
ANTWERP BELGIUM

Carrying the clubland atmosphere onwards, we chose rich, warm colours for the bedroom. The room is small and cosy, yet has been given grand treatment with the generous use of the two comfortable red patterns in burgundy, tan and navy blue – an important colour theme for 1986.

With its Victorian man's dressing mirror on an elaborate stand (picture 2), and the pile of battered old leather suitcases, this room looks as if it could well belong to a nineteenth century traveller, rather than to a twentieth century company man, who finds he is quite at home among the patterns and paraphernalia of yesterday, like the paisley curtain pattern, which is perennially popular all over the world.

The vogue for this highly recognisable pattern started in the late eighteenth century when travellers to India came home with beautiful, expensive shawls hand-woven in Kashmir. So popular were these that the East India Company started importing them. Then the idea was taken up by a weaver in Edinburgh who wanted to copy the shawls less expensively for mass production. The cheapest labour he was able to find was in the Scottish town of Paisley, where he set up a factory in 1805. The pine cone motif was copied on to woollen shawls, worn by the Victorian ladies of Europe

1▼   2▶

and America over their voluminous crinoline dresses. So popular did these shawls become that the Indian pattern lost its Eastern connotation and to this day is known almost universally as 'paisley'.

Country furnishing cotton in this classic pattern is used for the curtains with their richly draped pelmet, edged with thick bullion fringe, dyed in a tan colour. Like the pelmet in the drawing room this is also three pieces of fabric, the joins being under the diagonal rope trimming on the pelmet corners. The curtain fabric is Laura Ashley's Grand Paisley, lined with a co-ordinating oakleaf fabric which is also used for the bedroom walls.

For the bed (picture 1) we made a warm quilted bedspread from Laura Ashley Grand Paisley fabric. The comfortable rug folded on the end of the bed is also by Laura Ashley. The cushion is an antique one in colours that blend with the warm burgundy and tans.

The antique mahogany elbow chair (picture 3) has its seat upholstered in Grand Paisley fabric and trimmed with braid. The pleated bed valance is our plain burgundy country furnishing cotton and the bedspread is edged in navy blue.

The idea for the Oak Leaves pattern on the vinyl wallcovering (pictures 4 and 7) came from a fragment of a dress fabric made in the early nineteenth century. Laura Ashley has been collecting antique textiles for some years, many picked up in market stalls. These she uses when she wants to create traditional designs.

3▼

4▲   5▼ 6▼

With the Oak Leaves the scale of the pattern was enlarged and colours introduced that were felt to be right for the 1980s. In matching wallpaper and fabric, this is an ideal choice for the rich colourings of the bedroom.

From antique markets and shops, the small prints and silhouettes in their original dark frames sit comfortably against the oakleaf stripes of the vinyl wallcovering. The old tapestry bellpull (picture 7) with its elaborate handle is another antique market find.

You would find the bolster on the bed and bordered cushion easy to make (picture 5). The bolster is a sausage shape of cotton, stuffed with kapok. The cover is made from a cylinder of the paisley fabric, lined with plain tan Laura Ashley country furnishing cotton at each end. The cracker effect is made by pulling in the ends tightly by binding them with cord. Blue piping neatens off the cushion ends. The cover is made with a zip in the back so it can be taken off and washed. For one of the cushions, tan coloured country furnishing cotton piped in navy blue was used. A snippet of the linear oakleaf design was hemmed round the edges as a colourful border. A second cushion was added in the Grand Paisley design, also piped in navy blue. The circular tablecloth beside the bed, was made from country furnishing cotton in the same tan colour as the cushion. The photograph frame with its matching sand base colour is from the Desk Collection.

The extravagant-looking curtains (picture 6) are made from Grand Paisley and lined with the Oak Leaves fabric, which makes an interesting border when the curtains are looped back. As an extravagant touch we used tie-backs with heavy tassels on rope. Picture 8 shows the two patterns working together in the corner of the room with the tilting circular looking-glass above the old-fashioned ivory-topped bottles and dressing table accessories.

Curtains in Country Furnishing Cotton, Grand Paisley, Multi Burgundy with Oak Leaves, Multi Burgundy.

Vinyl Wallcovering is Oak Leaves, Multi Burgundy.

Quilted Bedspread and Bolster in Country Furnishing Cotton, Grand Paisley, Multi Burgundy edged in plain Navy.

Elbow Chair in Country Furnishing Cotton, Grand Paisley, Multi Burgundy, finished with braid, Dark Green/Burgundy/Sand.

Bed Valance in plain Country Furnishing Cotton, Burgundy.

Cushion in plain Country Furnishing Cotton, Tan, with Appliquéd Border made from Oak Leaves, Multi Burgundy.

Square Piped Cushion, Grand Paisley, Multi Burgundy.

Circular Tablecloth, in plain Country Furnishing Cotton, Tan.

AN ENGLISHMAN ABROAD
BATHROOM
GENTLEMAN'S APARTMENT
ANTWERP BELGIUM

This being an old-fashioned apartment, not surprisingly it has an old-fashioned bathroom. Before we decorated everything was white — the bath, the walls, the blinds. Advantages were the mahogany lavatory chair and the basin, built into a cupboard, but otherwise it all looked a bit stark — like something in those old black and white movies set in a dusty Victorian hotel. The lease specified that structural alterations were not allowed so the only way of making it comfortable was to introduce colour with the fabrics, wallpaper and paint.

The requirement was a place to relax with a good book in a steaming tub. The idea was to make a warm, rich-looking room.

The bath looked very stark painted white, so we decided to accentuate its age and shape. Inspiration for the stencil on the side came from a postcard of a Victorian bath by the English firm of Armitage. The card showed a century-old bath, decorated with an elaborate painted frieze. Using stencils, the splendid decoration in tan, sand and navy blue Laura Ashley paints was completed, then a coat of matt varnish added to make a tougher finish.

As the bathroom connects with the bedroom, we wanted to continue with the same colours in burgundy, tan and navy blue and the same paisley design, which comes in companion colourways, each with a different background.

Always having grand ideas, we decided to adapt an idea for a canopy we had seen on a Mediaeval bath in an English castle. This version is made from two lengths of our tan Grand Paisley hung from a grandiose gilded corona that had been found in an antique shop. The drapes were lined with more Grand Paisley in the deep blue background and bound together with plain navy blue.

A blind is always a practical choice for a bathroom window. This one is a sumptuous-looking festoon, edged in a six-inch navy blue bullion fringe. The woodwork in the room is painted navy blue, including the radiator cupboard.

The wallpaper is again in the same colours, but a small, Victorian pattern with a tan ground. Detail being all-important, the final touch was a wallpaper border in Trompe, neatening the contours of the room.

We selected fresh white paint for the cistern and pipework (picture 1), but went in quite the other direction for the rest of the room, wanting to introduce a feeling of relaxing warmth.

The textural wallpaper acts as a foil for the strongly patterned paisley fabric (picture 3). This close-up of the corner of the room illustrates how the various colours and patterns knit together. The festoon blind is Grand Paisley in tan with a heavy bullion fringe coloured to accentuate the navy blue in the paisley. The cushion is in a companion paisley in navy blue. The wallpaper border that runs down the edge of the window is an important detail. It works almost like a pencil outline, accentuating the contours of the room and sharpening up its shape.

The 'Mediaeval' corona (picture 2) is suspended from the ceiling. A castellated pelmet is braided in navy blue making a neat tent-like finish to the canopy over the bath.

Picture 4 shows how the curtains frame the bath – a little like one of those tented day-beds that were all the rage in the days of the Emperor Napoleon.

To give balance the bath curtains (picture 6) are edged with navy blue braid, matching the feet of the bath, painted in navy blue.

We designed the wallpaper (picture 5) to work with the two paisleys. The small Victorian print is restful and not too intrusive as a pattern.

1▲

2▲   3▼

Bath painted in Tan, Sand and Navy Flat Paints.

Bath Canopy in Country Furnishing Cotton, Grand Paisley, Multi Tan and lined in Grand Paisley, Multi Navy.

Festoon Blind in Country Furnishing Cotton, Grand Paisley, Multi Tan.

Woodwork in Navy Flat Paint

Wallpaper is Shamrock, Burgundy/Dark Green/Tan and **Wallpaper Border**, Trompe, Navy/Sand.

4▲ 5▼ 6▼

AN ENGLISHMAN ABROAD
KITCHEN
GENTLEMAN'S APARTMENT
ANTWERP BELGIUM

The comforting warm colours of old oak and mahogany combine with the practicality of new tiled surfaces to make this kitchen into a highly efficient yet friendly room.

A kitchen does not have to look clinical to work well. This one, with the feeling of one of those old butlers' pantries in a 1930s novel, is a place to inspire all sorts of good cooking and recipe trials. It's a place to forget the bustle of today, with no stark white surfaces or glaring spotlights. Yet it contains the necessities that modern kitchen life decrees, with all the cooking machines humming quietly away in their place.

Whilst this room demonstrates that an efficient kitchen need be neither spartan nor hospital-white, it also shows the great adaptability of Laura Ashley's favourite sprig patterns, which can be tailored beautifully to suit a masculine kitchen.

The art of making these patterns work is in choosing the right background colours. Here the creamy background colour gives a warm appearance on the tiles, vinyl wallcovering and the brown of the oak and mahogany furniture. The border paper outlines the contours of the room, separating the tiles from the wallpaper above, while a Roman blind is always ideal in a kitchen setting.

Roman Blind made in Bembridge, Burgundy/Navy/Sand.
Vinyl Wallcovering is Bembridge, Burgundy/Navy/Sand.
Wallpaper Border Swinburne, Burgundy/Navy/Sand.
Square Piped Cushions in Country Furnishing Cotton, Bembridge, Burgundy/Navy/Sand.
Floor Tiles (20 x 20 cm) Bembridge, Burgundy/Navy/Sand.
Wall Tiles (15 x 15 cm) Bembridge, Burgundy/Navy/Sand.

DINING ROOM

TOWN HOUSE

FLORIDA

The beautiful climate of Florida attracts people from all over the world, who love the kind January sunshine and the long sandy shores. The social season is from January to Easter when people fly in for polo, charity balls and auctions. From South America, especially, they come to Miami to do their shopping in one of the world's smartest international shopping centres.

Ever since the Spanish conquistadores first explored Florida in search of the fountain of youth, the influence of Spain has been strong. It's in the architecture that you notice it most.

At the turn of the century the gifted architect Addison Mizner was working in Florida, particularly in Palm Beach. A passionate admirer of Spanish and Italian architecture, he realised these styles would suit perfectly the climate in Florida. His houses are now much prized and the decorated rooms shown here are from a house of his School.

The blue of the Florida sky and the Atlantic seaboard spills indoors here – into the dining room with its vivid blue sofa and curtains, into the drawing room with the softer sky blues of early morning, and into the bedroom.

People love giving parties, especially informal ones, and the small dining room (pictured on the right) is where the ladies gather for lunch rather than using the large, formal dining room.

Here the blues of Florida invade the house. Selecting from our newest prints, we started with the curtain fabric, a cheerful chintz called Carousel, then worked in the rest of the room.

The walls are painted sapphire blue, then a white wooden trellis placed over them, to give the effect of a conservatory, with the diamond patterning at the window helping to filter through the bright sunlight outside, throwing soft shadows on the tiled floor. Trellises are used to great effect in Florida.

Plain sapphire blue glazed chintz was used for the sofa and the seats of these reproduction Italian dining chairs with their shell backs. Using the colours of the flowered fabric as a basis, cushions were added in blue and a matching bright poppy red, plus a table slip cover and napkins, picking out the buttermilk colour.

These cool blues and the lightness of the glazed chintz make the room shimmer in the evening, candlelit from the huge, romantic candelabra as seen on page 18. The final effect is friendly and casual yet stunning, so the hostess can rest assured that enough excitement is created. It's in a small extra dining room such as this, where the time spent is limited, that one can really have fun and use the boldest colour combinations.

Spanish-style doors lead into the dining room (picture 1). Using an abundance of fabric in the curtains with their thickly gathered pelmets (picture 3) helped to give the room a feeling of extravagance.

On the cool-looking floor are plain white tiles. A sensible and practical choice for summer rooms, they help to give a soothing appearance, as well as being cool to walk on, even on the hottest of days.

The frilled pelmets (picture 3) are simple to make. Strips of fabric have a channel sewn near the top on the reverse side. The pelmets are then gathered on to a curtain rod — quicker and easier than dealing with heading tape and hooks. They are also easy to remove for washing.

Today, decorating is becoming reminiscent of more adventurous times when pattern was mixed with pattern, like the cushions shown here. Details like bright red piping, used to marry different elements together, work well; while the cushion in the front of the picture is in the pretty floral Carousel print, the other two are in Palmetto — a favourite print, here in a new blue colourway.

Linear patterns like the flower print that climbs in a garland up the fabric in the dining room were fashionable in the last century. Traditional sprigs of flowers are translated into the design language of the 1980s by use of vivid colours — a point that makes this fabric especially adaptable for rooms of all kinds.

Curtains in Chintz, Carousel, Mustard Multi Sapphire.

Sofa in plain Chintz, Sapphire.

Dining Chair Seats in plain Chintz, Sapphire.

Circular Tablecloth in Chintz, Carousel, Mustard Multi Sapphire.

Square Table Slip Cover & Napkins in plain Chintz, Buttermilk.

Square Piped Cushions made in Chintz, Carousel, Mustard Multi Sapphire; plain Chintz, Poppy; and Country Furnishing Cotton, Palmetto, Denim/Tropical Green/White.

1◄ 2▼ 3▼

DRAWING ROOM
TOWN HOUSE
FLORIDA

This drawing room is typical of the Addison Mizner School: elements from the salon of a Florentine villa vie with the Spanish floor tiles. The lovely bleached panelling is in Floridian pecky cypress, so called because of its natural effect as if a giant bird had pecked it. This wood is now rather rare but was used greatly by Mizner.

The generous proportions of this room are remarkable and the house itself is listed as being of Historic Interest. It was therefore a labour of love to produce new prints and colours to harmonise with these surroundings. Rather than choosing very bright colours, soft blending shades were used so that a quiet restful atmosphere ensued for reading or other calm pursuits.

So the point of departure for the colour scheme was the new Chinoiserie chintz, used for the cushions on the sofa and chairs.

For hundreds of years Westerners have borrowed Oriental design ideas. It started in the seventeenth century when travellers began to bring back all kinds of imports from the East – silk, enamels and especially porcelain. These became so fashionable that in the eighteenth century Europeans started imitating Oriental design in architecture and all kinds of designs for the home. The style was romantic, echoing the rococo era with its elegant swirls and delicate humour. The style is called, like the chintz here, Chinoiserie.

The stylised Chinese scene with the pagoda in the background and the two figures chatting under a tree is typical of the eighteenth century conception of what China might look like. It is a calm, gentle pattern, smartened up by the stripes, which lends itself particularly well to fabric design.

Colours in the cushions were pulled out for use in the other elements of the room. The chairs and sofa are covered in two new fabrics: a textured dobby weave upholstered fabric in a soft shade of buttermilk and another upholstery weight fabric in a Chinese fretwork design. A clever idea here was to abut the two chairs together to form a seat which can be used as a double or two single chairs, as the mood takes you, and which extends the conversational areas in the room.

This maze-like pattern with its satisfying intermingling of lines first appeared thousands of years ago on Chinese bronze vessels. Ever since then it has inspired designers, lending itself especially well to use in this new fabric, where the geometric linear design makes a perfect foil for the cheerful Chinoiserie of the cushions.

1▲   2▼

The fretwork fabric is also used on the regal, draped curtain pelmets, with their long fringed side drapery. This window treatment is inspired by the ideas of the interior designers of the early nineteenth century, when it was high fashion to use two or more complementary fabrics together, elegantly looped back and edged with decorative fringes.

The grand chandelier and glistening French wall sconces give the room an elegant sparkle throughout the day, but most especially in the evening (picture 3). A view across to the fireplace shows how the patterns and plains in the blue and buttermilk colour scheme marry together. The curtains (picture 2) are straightforward to make. A deep bullion fringe edges the antique French carved pelmet board. The draped pelmet in our new Chinese fretwork design is made from three pieces of fabric.

3▲   4▼

The centre piece is gathered on each side and again in the centre of the window, then edged with bullion fringe to add to the rich effect. In one corner of the room reflected in the mirror (picture 3) is a circular table covered in pale blue country furnishing cotton, as are the lampshades. Cushions on the sofa in the new Chinoiserie fabric (picture 4) show how the colours are linked together.

Curtain Pelmets in Country Furnishing Cotton, Fretwork, Multi Smoke.

Sofa & Armchair in plain Dobby, Buttermilk.

Two Chairs abutted in Country Furnishing Cotton, Fretwork, Multi Smoke.

Square Piped Cushions made in Chintz, Chinoiserie, Kingfisher Multi Stone; Country Furnishing Cotton, Fretwork, Multi Smoke; and plain Country Furnishing Cotton, Buttermilk.

Tablecloth made in Country Furnishing Cotton, Fretwork, Multi Smoke.

Pleated Lampshades Fretwork, Multi Smoke.

1◄

6▲

HALL

This spacious hall with its black and white tiles is a room for grand theatrical effects. A room where you can make a real entrance in film star style.

Two of our new prints were chosen (picture 1). The classic striped fabric in grey and white is a new print — at home here in cool marble and black and white, even wrapped round the antique statue. But this stripe would be easily applicable in all sorts of other settings from traditional to contemporary.

On the table with its draped cloth (pictures 2 and 4) is the new Chinese fretwork fabric in crimson and grey. The cloth has a thick piped edge running round the table to give a more interesting finish. On the table is a collection of reproduction antique Greek vases. The candelabra and lantern behind it are of Spanish ironwork whilst the painting is after a seventeenth century original.

Window treatments on a stairway are not always easy to handle. Our solution (picture 5) shows how draped pelmets can add shape to the plain windows. Here, once again, the fabric is the Chinese fretwork design.

Formal rooms like this benefit from a balanced formal arrangement (picture 6). Thick rope is used on the stairs, tied to antique bronze lions.

A closer view of the grey striped fabric is shown in picture 8. The curtains are gathered on poles across the arched windows. This formal grey and white striped fabric makes an ideal background for the antique sculptures, while the busier pattern of the Chinese fretwork fabric on the table adds rich colour which blends in happily.

Picture 9 shows how the circular table with its colourful cloth makes an eye-catching central hub for the lofty arched room.

3▲

2▲

7▲

4▲ 5▼

8▲ 9▼

Curtains in Country Furnishing Cotton, Cirque, Grey/White.

Curtains on stairway, in Country Furnishing Cotton, Oriana, Multi Crimson.

Tablecloth made in Country Furnishing Cotton, Oriana, Multi Crimson.

VERANDAH

TOWN HOUSE

FLORIDA

The sub-tropical flowers of Florida are a feast of colour. In this verandah where house meets garden, we decided to use soft beiges and pinks for the blinds and cushions, as a foil for the colours of the hydrangeas and other exotic flowers outside.

With all the bright sunlight, window blinds are essential. These huge Roman shades make an attractive answer because they pull up into elegant folds, while by day the fabric colours give the room a delightful coolness.

The huge fan and cane chairs create an exotic, Indian atmosphere, conjuring up a feeling of nostalgia for the bygone days of the Raj.

While the cotton fabric for the blinds and the fitted cushions is in a quiet pattern called Attic, its companion for the brighter cushions is more striking. In this design, Indienne, a café au lait ground is scattered with delicate flowers in blues and pinks.

The rich pinks on the cushion fabrics are an almost exact match for the lush pots of hydrangeas that flourish happily in the warmth of Florida's climate.

1▲ 2▼ 3▼ 4▶

If you have ever wanted to know what a lounge lizard looks like, picture 1 gives the answer. Lewis, the pet iguana, is exploring the cushions on the verandah. But rather than paying too much attention to Lewis, look closely, and study how happily the two fabrics used in this room work together and how the plain burgundy piping on the flowery cushions gives a neat finish.

Piping is again the thing to look at on the cushions in picture 2. Some are completed in self-piping and others in a bright white.

The diamond trellis is used to decorate a bench seat with the cushions covered in the two side-by-side cottons.

A small antique wall trough of carved stone contains a drinking fountain. Trellis work at the arched windows gives an Indian effect. The long bench by the verandah window covered in the Attic fabric, doubles as a bed so that the room can be used as a sleeping porch whenever extra visitors arrive.

Blind in Country Furnishing Cotton, Attic, Mulberry/Sand/White.

Daybed & Fitted Chair Cushions in Country Furnishing Cotton, Attic, Mulberry/Sand/White.

Square Piped Cushions made in Country Furnishing Cotton, Indienne, Multi Allspice.

5▲

BEDROOM
TOWN HOUSE
FLORIDA

The opulent carved antique four-poster bed demands that the fabrics in this bedroom should possess a certain flamboyance. The rich crimson of the furnishing cotton goes well with the deeply polished wood of the bed, the warmth of the red being softened by the pale jade and buttermilk of the sofa and its cushions. The bed itself was discovered in Jamaica.

Inspiration for the flowered Chinoiserie fabric came from Crace's designs for the Prince Regent's famous Royal Pavilion at Brighton. These designs were drawn up in 1803 and typify the traditional flowers so loved in English furnishing fabrics.

The richly gathered curtains are topped by plain pelmets. These are quite simple to copy: using a pelmet board, a layer of wadding is tacked under the Chinoiserie fabric to give a rich, padded effect.

Our new Chinese fretwork design in the buttermilk colourway was used for the accessories – the sofa and its frilled cushions (pictures 2 and 3). The best thing about both of the printed cottons in this room is their versatility of co-ordination, allowing different colours to be played up or down, depending on the demands of different locations.

1▲ 2▼ 3▶

Curtains in Chintz, Crystal, Crimson Multi White.

Bedspread made in Chintz, Crystal, Crimson Multi White.

Square Piped Cushions made in Chintz, Crystal, Crimson Multi White; Country Furnishing Cotton, Petra, Jade; and Country Furnishing Cotton, Petra, Crimson.

Square Frilled Cushions made in Country Furnishing Cotton, Fretwork, Multi Buttermilk.

Pleated Lampshades Fretwork, Multi Buttermilk.

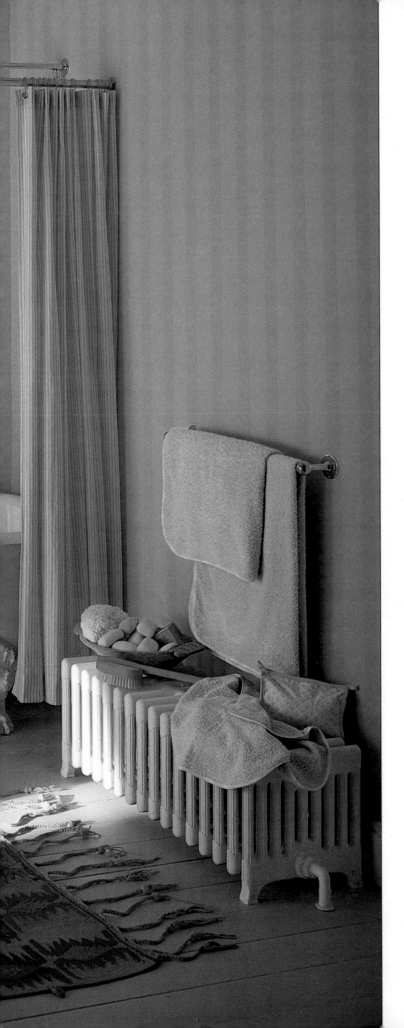

BATHROOM

FARMHOUSE

NORTHERN ENGLAND

Be bold with paint. That is the decoration message of this bathroom with its cheerful stripes of apricot and aquamarine. Paint colours are tied in with the Roman blind, made from a new cotton in a splashy pastel print. The floor is painted with white gloss.

For the stripes, we first painted all over with apricot. Then, using a plumb line to make sure the verticals were correct, we marked out the stripes and when the paint was dry applied strips of special 'masking' tape. This is a sticky tape, designed to be easy to remove. Next, we painted the aquamarine stripes. The sticky tape made sure the edges of the lines were neat and did not blot the apricot. When the aquamarine dried, we removed the tape. Final touch was a lick of white for the 1930s Lloyd loom chair and a cushion to match the blind.

The white skirting and window add to the fresh, airy look, while the aquamarine painted bath blends agreeably with the colour scheme.

Walls in stripes of Soft Apricot Emulsion and Light Aquamarine Emulsion Paint.

Roman Blind in Country Furnishing Cotton, Emma, Multi Apricot/White.

Shower Curtain made in Country Furnishing Cotton, Brighton Rock, Aquamarine/White using Shower Curtain Kit.

Chair Cushion in Country Furnishing Cotton, Emma, Multi Apricot/White.

Loom Chair in White Emulsion Paint.

Floorboards in White Gloss Paint.

Bath in Light Aquamarine Emulsion Paint.

Towels Aquamarine bound with Regency Stripe, Apricot/Aquamarine/White.

Cosmetic Bag & Tissue Box Cover Palmetto, Aquamarine/Apricot/White. (Not available by post.)

CREAM
RHUBARB
SEA SALT
CABBAGE
BRAN
HONEY

KITCHEN
PERIOD COTTAGE
HOME COUNTIES ENGLAND

Whether it's a matter of a patiently cooked steamed pudding or a hasty omelette, this kitchen, with its cheerful tiled walls and floor, is a room to enjoy.

The bright pattern on these new tiles is called Pavilion. The coloured corners can be combined in different ways: the tiles on the walls are laid to give solid blue and green diamonds; on the floor they are put together differently, giving solid red and yellow diamonds. Picking out the green in the tiles we painted the shelves in our own Moss paint, adding a collection of old circular bread boards to make a frieze on the top shelf.

Curtains in Country Furnishing Cotton, Marquee, Denim/White.
Floor Tiles (20 x 20 cm) Pavilion, Poppy/Mustard/Apple/Denim.
Wall Tiles (15 x 15 cm) Pavilion, Poppy/Mustard/Apple/Denim.
Shelves in Moss, Gloss paint.
Apron & Oven Glove Marquee, Denim/White.
Laura Ashley China Scottish Thistle.

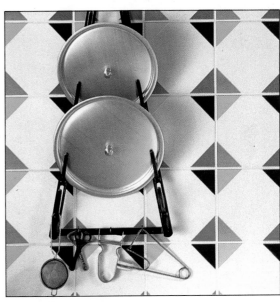

SCULLERY

FARMHOUSE

MID-WALES

The clean, fresh crispness of black and white is the keynote for this simple scullery in a Welsh farmhouse.

We wanted to cheer the room up, yet to preserve the feeling of the spick-and-span dairy, needed for a room where butter and cheese is made and freshly picked vegetables brought in from the garden.

The new wallpaper is based on an early nineteenth century dress print called Cherries, while the neat striped fabric is a favourite ticking newly printed in black and white.

Curtains and Chair Cushion in Country Furnishing Cotton, Marquee, Black/White.

Wallpaper is Cherries, Black/White.

Woodwork in White Gloss Paint.

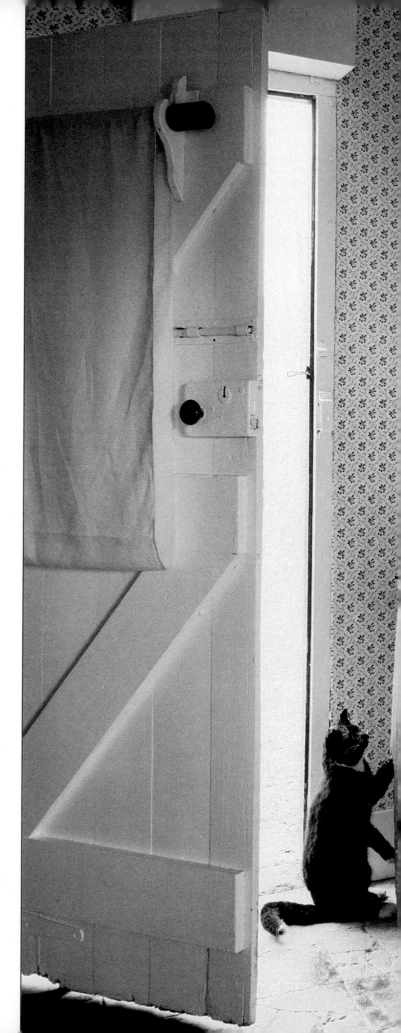

BEDROOM
FARMHOUSE
MID-WALES

This is the sort of bedroom that every daughter dreams of. It's in the attic of a Welsh farmhouse, yet for all the world could have come straight out of a nineteenth century children's story illustration by Kate Greenaway.

Little girls love to have bedrooms that are pretty and feminine and this new print, with its matching vinyl wallcovering, is just right for a picture book effect. The draped bed, lined in rose pink; the generously gathered curtains with a bow on the pelmet board; all this, added to the vinyl wallcovering, creates a charming atmosphere fit only for the very best behaved young ladies.

Interior decoration today is more flexible than ever before. Wider colour palettes are used, giving much greater choice. It is not merely curtains that match wallcoverings; co-ordination goes all through the room, including the bedspread and even the lining of the antique doll's pram. Small details are much more carefully thought out — like the bows for example. It's these touches that make a room look special.

Sara Jane is the highly appropriate name for the new print we used in the bedroom. The pattern is inspired by an eighteenth century French design. For centuries the pretty flowered designs of France have been loved the world over. Their famous *toiles* (French for cloth) have adorned all sorts of interiors from the grandest of châteaux to the most unassuming country cottages.

Decorating details to remember are the way the pink fabric in a soft wickerwork pattern is used to line the bed curtains and bedspread, and to cover the chair, the pillows and frilled cushions.

Sitting quietly on the floor is the owner of the room holding her teddy bear, another new addition to our collection, as are the tapestry cushions on her cot, and the little tapestry pin cushion in the doll's pram.

1▲   2▲   3▶

Because it contains an assortment of colours, this print and its matching wallpaper can be used in all sorts of different ways. The final effect depends on which of the particular colours in the pattern you choose to emphasise. In this case we chose the pink, patterned on the linings and pillows (pictures 1 and 2), and plain as edging on the curtains and tie-backs.

In the picture on the left, the little fabric covered sewing boxes are a new idea for us. They have padded tops for pins and contain sewing essentials – scissors, a plait of threads, pins and needles and a measuring tape.

The bed hangings are simple to make (picture 1), just two straight lengths of the flowery fabric, lined with the soft rose patterned cotton and edged in plain rose pink. These are gathered onto a circular corona above the bed. For the bedspread, one width of the flowery fabric was lined with pink and interlined with warm wadding, then quilted, using a quilting foot on the home sewing machine.

The row of dolls naturally are dressed in Laura Ashley fabrics, the two antique ones are wearing a new light cotton lawn called Kate.

Heaped on the little Victorian chair (picture 2) is a clan of teddy bears and their friends. The chair and frilled cushion are covered in the same rose pink fabric, but the cushion has a smoke-coloured piping, a neat finish to link it to yet another colour in the flowered vinyl wallcovering and curtains.

Curtains in Country Furnishing Cotton,
Sara Jane, Kingfisher Multi Stone.

Bedspread & Drape in Country Furnishing Cotton,
Sara Jane, Kingfisher Multi Stone.

Lining Fabric for Drape in Country Furnishing Cotton,
Wickerwork, White/Rose.

Vinyl Wallcovering Sara Jane, Kingfisher Multi Stone.

Pillowslip made in Country Furnishing Cotton,
Wickerwork, White/Rose.

Armchair & Round Frilled Cushion
made in Country Furnishing Cotton, Wickerwork, White/Rose.

Cushions made from Tapestry Sewing Kits,
Morning Parlour, Deep Sapphire Multi White; Kew Gardens,
Mint Multi White; Blue Ribbons, Smoke Multi Stone.

Pin Cushion made from Tapestry Sewing Kit,
Kate, Rose/Moss/White

Pin Cushion Boxes Brighton Rock, Sugar Pink/White;
Kate, Sugar Pink/White.

Antique Dolls' Dresses in Country Furnishing Cotton,
Kate, Rose/Moss/White.

CONSERVATORY

CHATEAU

PICARDY NORTHERN FRANCE

In a conservatory the house meets the garden, making an ideal place for alfresco meals. This beautiful conservatory, designed about one hundred years ago, is attached to a château in Picardy, Northern France.

What we wanted here, was to choose a fabric that would echo the flowery profusion of the garden, be in keeping with the room, yet be peaceful and not too dominant in colour.

The solution was our well-loved country furnishing cotton, which looks quite hand-painted here with its sweet, almost naïve pattern of flowers and ribbons caught up in bows.

This is another example of interpreting the feeling of yesterday's designs to the present day. Ribbons were often used on early nineteenth century fabrics and this one is based on one of these historic designs. Unlike some of the early ninteenth century designs which feature busy, crowded small flowers, this has a relaxed free-hand design.

Enormously adaptable, this design would be at home in a drawing room, bedroom or dining room just as much as it is on the tablecloth and chair cushions here.

The fabric, being a colourful one, has lots of different co-ordination possibilities and we chose the terracotta, picked out on the border of the tablecloth, on the cushion piping and in the cream and terracotta mats on the table, from our Dining Collection.

Circular cloths are simple to sew. Make a square of fabric that measures the same length as the diameter of the table plus twice its height. If you need more than one width of fabric, use one width for the centre and add half a width to the two sides to make the square large enough — this way you don't get a seam running down the centre of the cloth. Then mark out the circle and finish off the cut edges with a contrasting border.

Quite apart from being pretty, the circular tablecloth is practical too because it's easy to wash. It turns a relaxed eating corner into somewhere much more romantic; a place for soothing cups of tea after croquet on the lawn, for strawberries and cream, or a quiet supper in the summer.

With its grand doorway this French conservatory is an ideal place for growing tender plants. It is also a quiet retreat at any time of the day – a colourful corner to hide with a good book, to sit and chat or to have tea.

The open doors invite visitors to an enticing table setting (picture 1) with the prettily draped table and comfortably cushioned chairs.

Waiting on a tray are the ingredients for afternoon tea French style – delicious summer *tarte aux fraises*, lashings of cream and under the cosy a steaming hot pot of tea. The tea cosy, the napkins and the table mat are all from our Dining Collection. On the shelf behind is an old-fashioned wicker basket, lined with fabric to match the tablecloth. This is an attractive idea and easy to copy. A neat terracotta coloured bow just completes the effect.

There is something much more comfortable about a cushion with a frill. It gives a feminine finish and is also easy to make at home. An important design detail is the use of piping on the cushion which picks up the terracotta colour in the fabric as well as being a perfect match with the napkins and table mats.

Tablecloth and cushions (picture 4), combined with the sharpness of the terracotta, make an ideal partnership.

Tablecloth in Country Furnishing Cotton, Maypole, Terracotta Multi Cream.

Chair Cushions & Square Frilled Cushions in Country Furnishing Cotton, Maypole, Terracotta Multi Cream.

Napkins, Place Mats, Tea Cosy, Milfoil, Cream/Terracotta.

BATHROOM
COUNTRY HOUSE
WEST COUNTRY ENGLAND

Sapphire blue and sparkling white make the freshest of colour combinations in this bathroom where we mixed our floor and wall tiles with stripes and a prettily flowered fabric. Using the blue and white floor tiles diagonally breaks up the rather square lines of this small room. Notice too, how the blue border tiles that edge the floor and bath are also used as a border on the walls — a clever idea to copy. On the walls above is a softly patterned ticking design vinyl wallcovering, with the bolder Regatta stripe being used for the window seat cushion. The bright blue cushions in plain chintz add more bold squares of colour to contrast with the white.

Floor Tiles (20 x 20cm) plain Sapphire and White.
Wall Tiles (15 x 15cm) plain Sapphire and White.
Border Tiles (8 x 4cm) Sapphire.
Vinyl Wallcovering is Candy Stripe, Sapphire/White.
Vinyl Wallcovering on Bath is Kate, Sapphire/Apple/White.
Curtains for Wash-basin in Country Furnishing Cotton, Kate, Sapphire/Apple/White.
Window Seat Cushion in Country Furnishing Cotton, Regatta, Sapphire/White.
Armchair in Country Furnishing Cotton, Kate, Sapphire/Apple/White with Cushion made from Tapestry Sewing Kit, Morning Parlour, Deep Sapphire Multi White.
Square Piped Plain Chintz Cushions Sapphire.
Round Frilled Cushions made in Country Furnishing Cotton, Kate, Sapphire/Apple/White.
Towels Sapphire bound in Regatta, Sapphire/White.

Transform any room with floral garlands, smart stripes or a simple trellis. Vinyl wallcovering and wallpaper for 1986. Page 52.

Crisp, clean and hardwearing. The exclusive qualities of linen are now combined with the softness of pure cotton in linen union. Page 66.

Country house sophistication captured in a fabric. Chintz in three new designs and five new plain colours. Discover the brilliance of traditional glazed cotton. Page 70.

The finishing touch of decorative trimmings. Braid, fringing, binding, gimp and tie-backs provide subtle additions which make all the difference. Page 80.

The natural qualities of pure cotton give Laura Ashley country furnishing cotton its unique character. Page 56.

The answer to household wear and tear is a strong, hardwearing fabric for upholstery. A tough, plain-weave cotton — upholstery fabric. Page 68.

All the charm of Laura Ashley's prints and colours in a water-resistant, plastic covered fabric, perfect for kitchen, bathroom or nursery. Page 74.

Decorators know the secret of paint. Simple, quick and bold, with the power to create an instant interior. Every colour creates a different mood. Express yourself in paint. Page 82.

A fine satin finish is the feature of Laura Ashley drawing room fabric, recalling as it does the cotton sateen once found in every Victorian household. Page 62.

Surface texture gives added interest to a plain fabric. Dobby, the new heavyweight, woven upholstery fabric. Page 69.

Use borders to catch the eye. In paper and fabric, highlight the colours and prints featured on walls and furniture. Wallpaper and fabric borders. Page 75.

Splash back, wall or floor, tiles have so many uses. Laura Ashley ceramic tiles in prints and plains including the new four colour tile. Page 84.

THE ELEMENTS OF STYLE

Light up, and show off your room to its best advantage. Lampshades and lampbases designed to co-ordinate. Lighting. Page 88.

The look of luxury and the comfort of pure feather padding. The characteristic qualities of Laura Ashley cushions. A larger selection than ever before. Page 96.

Relax in the softness of Laura Ashley Burlington bedlinen. A wide choice of fully co-ordinated sheets, duvet covers, shams and dust ruffles. Page 102.

Individually finished furnishings. Made to Measure curtains, pelmets and blinds. Made to Measure upholstered furniture. Page 111.

A table for two, or three or four or more, decked with Laura Ashley's collection of tablecloths, hard and padded place-mats, and accessories. Dining Collection. Page 92.

The traditional warmth of a handmade patchwork quilt. Two distinctive styles complement the entire collection, giving any bedroom an atmosphere of luxury. Page 98.

Pretty useful. For desk top and bathroom. Collections of fabric-covered cosmetic bags, sewing boxes, picture frames, diaries and writing accessories. Page 108.

PRINT GUIDE

Scottish Thistle
F4 Navy/Sage/Sand   065562

Product Code: given in main copy	
Design: Scottish Thistle	
Design Number: F4	
Colourway: Navy/Sage/Sand	
Reference Number: 065562	

Crafty sew and sew. The Englishwoman's pastimes have always included embroidery and patchwork. Tapestry cushion kits and patch-work pieces. Page 95.

The delicate filigree of Nottingham Lace decorates panels at the window, tablecloth and bedspread. Pure white, and soft cream lace. Page 100.

Dry up with luxuriously soft towels, made by Burlington, in co-ordinating Laura Ashley colours, perfectly complementing the decoration of your bathroom. Page 110.

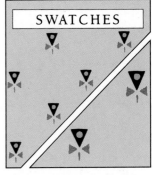

SWATCHES

In order to give a more realistic view of each print, and show as much as possible of the pattern repeat, all swatches are shown two-thirds actual size, unless otherwise stated. Although the colour reproduction throughout the magazine is as accurate as possible slight variations may occur.

51

WALL COVERINGS

In the fifteenth century painted papers were introduced as a substitute for expensive pictures and tapestry wall hangings.

Today their natural successor, printed wallpaper, perhaps with a co-ordinating border, is still the simplest means of giving additional interest to an otherwise plain room.

The subtle variations of form and colour twist and twine across the surface of the wall, or stand in regular formation, catching the eye, defining space, and providing playful illusions of depth, which fill the whole room with a previously unnoticed sense of proportion and light.

For 1986 Laura Ashley has taken the bold and unexpected step of converting 60 of our newest and most popular *wallpaper* patterns to a totally new *vinyl wallcovering*. Science and art have combined efforts successfully to provide you with a vinyl wallcovering that has a matte paper-like appearance but that is fully scrubbable (which wallpapers cannot be) and more durable. The purists among you may still choose from the additional 49 patterns in our collection that are produced on our classic high-quality washable wallpaper.

The symbol key below will make the distinction between our classic washable *wallpaper* and our new scrubbable *vinyl wallcovering*.

VINYL WALLCOVERING

Vinyl Wallcovering 53 cm (21 ins) wide. 10 yards per roll

Product Code *308* $19.50 per roll

WALLPAPER

Wallpaper 53 cm (21 ins) wide 10 yards per roll

Product Code *301* $17.50 per roll

Vinyl Wallcoverings are made in the U.K. Wallpaper is made in the U.K. and the Netherlands.

NEW WALL COVERINGS

This year sees the introduction of a number of new wall covering prints, from the enchanting simplicity of Shamrock to the light floral freshness of Emma, and the Chinoiseries of Petra and Pagoda.

Cherries F805 Black/White   *374027*

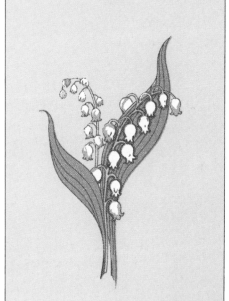

Lily of the Valley F487 Trop.Green Multi Stone   *093508*

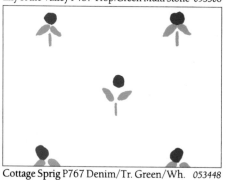

Cottage Sprig P767 Denim/Tr. Green/Wh.   *053448*

Trellis P768 Tropical Green/White   *054274*

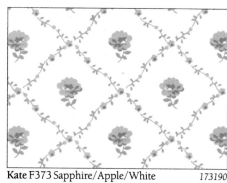

Kate F373 Sapphire/Apple/White   *173190*

Sweetbriar F388 Apricot Multi White   *179146*

Sara Jane F798 Kingfisher Multi Stone   *368479*

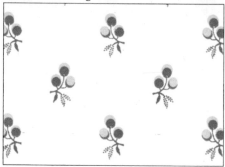

Rowan F686 Light Rose/Moss/White   *365533*

Sophie F614 Multi Straw/Cream   *352401*

Emma C17 Multi Straw/Cream   *517401*

Scottish Thistle F4 Navy/Sage/Sand   *065562*

Shamrock F711 Burgundy/Dk. Green/Tan   *375556*

Oak Leaves F785 Multi Burgundy   *364243*

Albert F288 Dark Green Multi Sage   *339563*

Rowan F686 Sage/Dark Green/Cream   *365554*

Cirque F782 Buttermilk   *371328*

Pagoda F809 Crimson Multi White   *378565*

Petra F671 Jade   *357339*

Bembridge F66 Burgundy/Navy/Sand   *132260*

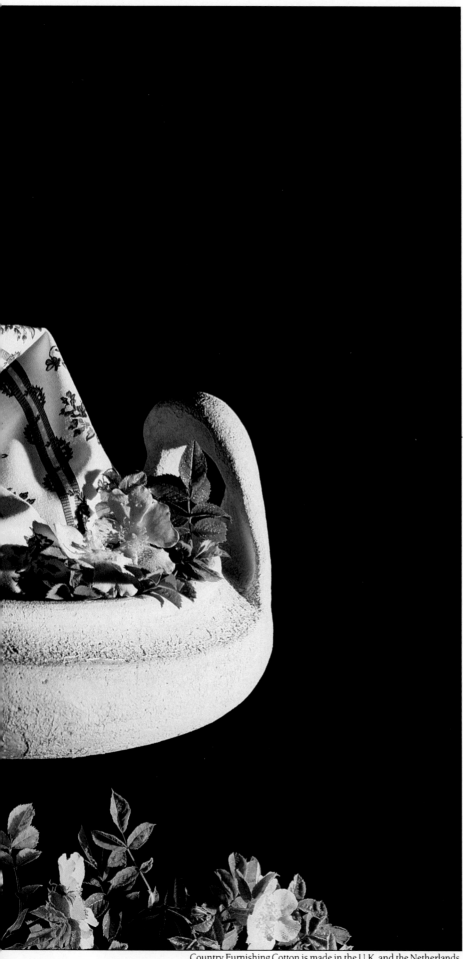

COUNTRY FURNISHING COTTON

Cotton furnishing fabrics have been a feature of the English country house since the seventeenth century. The phenomenal popularity of such printed cottons derives from the enduring qualities of the fabric itself: its natural softness, its unmistakeable classic look and feel, and its ability to take the bright colours so popular on English fabrics since the early 1700s.

Laura Ashley country furnishing cotton is made from pure cotton in a plain weave. It is printed exclusively by Laura Ashley in specially selected fade-resistant pigments, making it particularly suitable for use with a lining fabric on curtains and drapes.

Also recommended for use on roller blinds, festoon blinds and light upholstery.

Country Furnishing Cotton

Width: 122 cm (48 ins)
Max. continuous length: 35 yards
Washing: warm wash (40°C), or dry clean. Please allow for 3-5% shrinkage after the first wash. Do not bleach. Hot iron.

Product Code *201* $12.50 per yard

Country Furnishing Cotton is made in the U.K. and the Netherlands.

NEW COUNTRY FURNISHING COTTON

This year's new collection spans three continents. From India come exotic Paisleys in deep, masculine shades of dark green, navy blue and burgundy.

From the Far East, Regency Chinoiseries reflect all the opulence of the 1800s in new, muted tones of crimson, buttermilk and jade.

All the charm of Victorian rural life is evoked in a number of new prints ranging from the classic simplicity of black and white stripes and cherries to the hand-printed look of country florals such as Sara Jane and Maypole.

* Due to technical difficulties, the Fretwork design has been revised, and is now available as shown here.

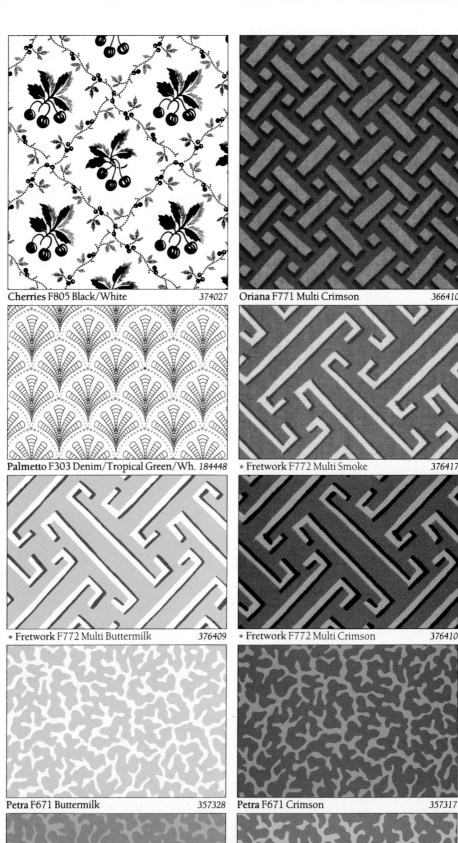

Cherries F805 Black/White   *374027*

Oriana F771 Multi Crimson   *366410*

Palmetto F303 Denim/Tropical Green/Wh. *184448*

* Fretwork F772 Multi Smoke   *376417*

* Fretwork F772 Multi Buttermilk   *376409*

* Fretwork F772 Multi Crimson   *376410*

Petra F671 Buttermilk   *357328*

Petra F671 Crimson   *357317*

Petra F671 Jade   *357339*

Petra F671 Moss   *357102*

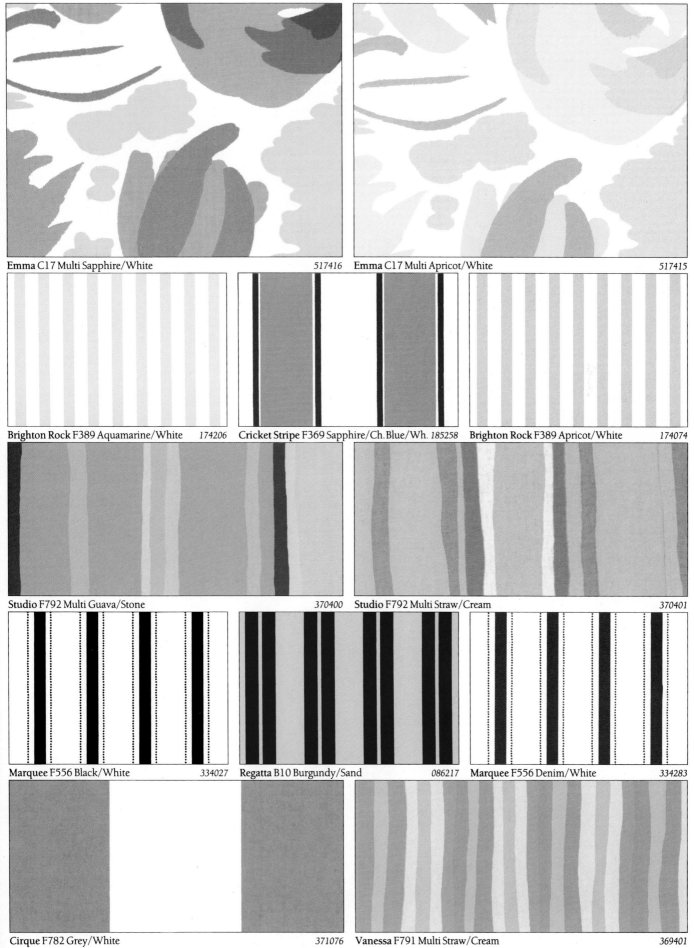

Emma C17 Multi Sapphire/White *517416*

Emma C17 Multi Apricot/White *517415*

Brighton Rock F389 Aquamarine/White *174206*

Cricket Stripe F369 Sapphire/Ch.Blue/Wh. *185258*

Brighton Rock F389 Apricot/White *174074*

Studio F792 Multi Guava/Stone *370400*

Studio F792 Multi Straw/Cream *370401*

Marquee F556 Black/White *334027*

Regatta B10 Burgundy/Sand *086217*

Marquee F556 Denim/White *334283*

Cirque F782 Grey/White *371076*

Vanessa F791 Multi Straw/Cream *369401*

Grand Paisley F706 Multi Navy *363413*

Grand Paisley F706 Multi Burgundy *363243*

Grand Paisley F706 Multi Tan *363411*

Bembridge F66 Burgundy/Navy/Sand *132260*

Paisley F477 Burgundy/Navy/Tan *332555*

Wood Violet P753 Terracotta/Moss/Cream *046270*

Oak Leaves F785 Multi Dark Green *364414*

Attic F572 Mulberry/Sand/White *367557*

Oak Leaves F785 Multi Burgundy *364243*

Rowan F686 Sage/Dark Green/Cream *365554*

Rowan F686 Light Rose/Moss/White *365533*

Sara Jane F798 Kingfisher Multi Stone *368479*

Maypole F634 Terracotta Multi Cream *385233*

Kate F373 Sapphire/Apple/White *173190*

NEW PLAIN COUNTRY FURNISHING COTTON

Colour	Code
Cream	020110
Buttermilk	020328
Sand	020109
Straw	020329
Tan	020122
Sugar Pink	020327
Guava	020330
Sage	020123
Apple	020103
Mustard	020118
Denim	020525
Navy	020104
Jade	020339
Dark Green	020101
Crimson	020317

LINING FABRIC

An indispensable accessory for all those who make curtains or blinds at home. Laura Ashley lining fabric is 100% cotton and produced using fade-resistant dyes, in a choice of cream or white.

Lining Fabric

Width: 122 cm (48 ins). Maximum continuous length: 50 yards
Washing: machine washable (40°C).
Please allow for 3-5% shrinkage after the first wash.

Product Code 206 $5.00 per yard

Lining Fabric is made in the U.S.A.

White	020100
Cream	020110

DRAWING ROOM FABRIC

Sophisticated cotton sateen was a hallmark of the late Victorian drawing room. Laura Ashley drawing room fabric, a heavyweight satin-weave cotton, has the same luxurious quality and soft, natural drape that characterised its nineteenth century predecessor.

This year sees three new introductions to the range: Regency Stripe in an elegant green and burgundy; Favorita on a navy ground, to co-ordinate perfectly with the range of Paisleys; and the Albert trellis in dark green and burgundy.

Particularly suitable for curtains and light upholstery, Laura Ashley drawing room fabric is printed in a width of 122 cm (48 ins), using high quality, light-resistant dyes.

Drawing Room Fabric

Width: 122 cm (48 ins)
Maximum continuous length: 35 yards
Washing: warm wash (40°C) or dry clean. Please allow for up to 5% shrinkage after the first wash.
Medium hot iron.

Product Code 215 $17.50 per yard

Please note that all drawing room fabric swatches are shown at 25% of their actual size.

Drawing Room Fabric is made in the Netherlands

Kew Gardens F484 Mint Multi White *090396*

Mr. Jones F381 Navy/Burgundy/Sand *190261*

Emperor F210 Navy Multi Stone *145231*

Michaelmas P769 Burgundy/Sand/White *055185*

Emmeline F127 Sand Multi White *147139*

Albert F288 Oak Multi Sand *339502*

Emperor F210 Terracotta Multi Cream *145233*

Garlands F340 Rose Multi Stone *177478*

Malcolm F403 Multi Cream *088395*

Regency Stripe F374 Dk. Green/Burg./Sand *197446*

Michaelmas P769 Plum/Sand/Cream *055223*

Albert F288 Dark Green Multi Sage *339563*

Venetia F99 Burgundy/Gold *146232*

Country Roses F430 Rose Multi White *089144*

Favorita F206 Dark Green Multi Navy *144564*

Clarissa F45 Apricot Multi White *076146*

Favorita F206 Navy Multi Sand *144480*

Favorita F206 Dark Green Multi Sand *144230*

LINEN UNION

It is probable that linen was in use at an even earlier date than cotton, possibly as far back as 2500 BC. The fine durable qualities of this cloth made it a commodity which came to be coveted by the most discerning of people.

With the expansion of the European weaving trade in Mediaeval times a cloth was introduced which combined the best qualities of both linen and its less expensive counterpart, cotton. In this tradition Laura Ashley has now developed a similar linen union fabric, which successfully interweaves the luxurious durability of linen with the crease-resistant properties of fine cotton.

This unique fabric, consisting of 60% linen and 40% cotton, is printed with pigment dyes selected for their light-resistant qualities, and is particularly suitable for use in upholstery.

Linen Union

Width: 140 cm (55 ins)
Max. continuous length: 25 yards
Dry clean only.

Product Code 224 $22.00 per yard

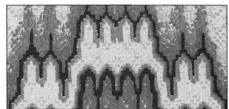

Florentina F358 Dk. Green Multi Stone   *192496*

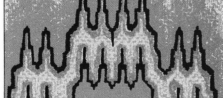

Florentina F358 Burgundy Multi Stone   *192481*

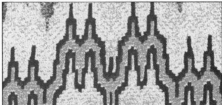

Florentina F358 Smoke Multi Cream   *192247*

Damask F526 Kingfisher/Smoke   *326281*

Damask F526 Dark Green/Mid Green   *326499*

Grapes F62 Smoke Multi Cream   *158247*

Linen Union is made in the U.K.

UPHOLSTERY FABRIC

In response to the demand for a hard-wearing fabric, suitable for all forms of upholstery, Laura Ashley have developed this strong, plain-weave cotton.

1986 sees the introduction of seven new prints including a strikingly bold free-hand pastel stripe, Studio, to complement the Emma and Sophie prints.

Upholstery Fabric

Width: 150 cm (59 ins)
Max. continuous length: 25 yards
Washing: warm wash (40°C) or dry clean. Do not bleach.
Medium to hot iron.

Product Code *209* $25.00 per yard

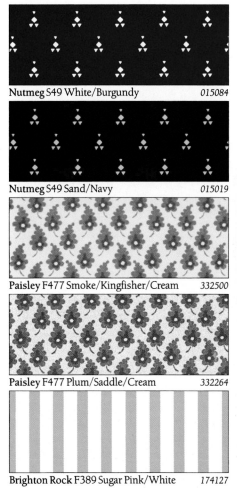

Nutmeg S49 White/Burgundy   *015084*

Nutmeg S49 Sand/Navy   *015019*

Paisley F477 Smoke/Kingfisher/Cream   *332500*

Paisley F477 Plum/Saddle/Cream   *332264*

Brighton Rock F389 Sugar Pink/White   *174127*

Kew Gardens F484 Mint Multi White   *090396*

Favorita F206 Dark Green Multi Sand   *144230*

Country Roses F430 Rose Multi White   *089144*

Emperor F210 Terracotta Multi Cream   *145233*

Studio F792 Multi Straw/Cream   *370401*

Emma C17 Multi Straw/Cream   *517401*

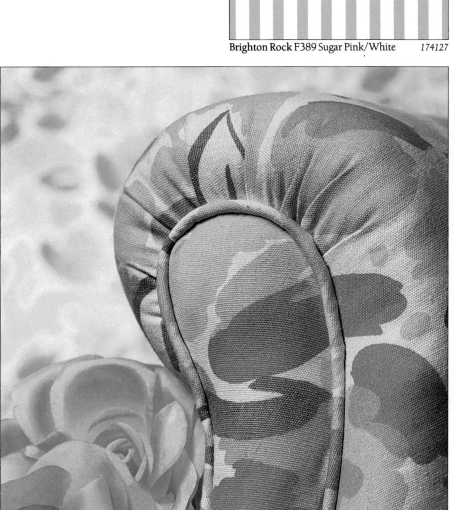

Cordelia F537 Multi Stone   328397

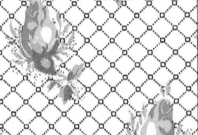

Favorita F206 Navy Multi Sand   144480

Rosamund F590 Rose Multi White   094144

Emperor F210 Navy Multi Stone   145231

Mr. Jones F381 Navy/Burgundy/Sand   190261

Palmetto F303 Dk.Green/Raspberry/Sand   184263

DOBBY

A plain coloured fabric can often make a refreshing change to the use of prints on upholstery and loose covers. This traditional dobby fabric with its small woven diamond motif originally achieved popularity in Europe in the mid-eighteenth century. Its subtle surface texture presents a look of understated opulence which will suit any chair or sofa. This new fabric, in hard-wearing pure cotton in one of seven colours or in its natural, untreated state, is strong enough for even the most frequent use.

Dobby

Width: 137 cm (54 ins)
Max. continuous length: 25 yards
Dry clean only.

Product Code 223 $18.00 per yard

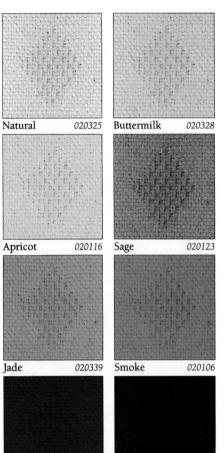

Natural	020325	Buttermilk	020328
Apricot	020116	Sage	020123
Jade	020339	Smoke	020106
Burgundy	020115	Navy	020104

Dobby is made in the U.K.

CHINTZ

Chintz. That most English of fabrics, perfectly evoking all the elegance and easy sophistication of country house life. Originally, chintzed cotton was manufactured in India for export to Europe where it has sustained its popularity since the seventeenth century.

Laura Ashley chintz is produced with a full glaze finish, making it quite as attractive as an antique original, adding a brilliance and lustre to any curtains, drapes, pelmets, blinds or light upholstery.

This year the collection is far larger than ever before, with three new designs and five plain colours to complement many other new prints in fabric and wall covering.

Chintz

Width: 120 cm (47 ins)
Maximum continuous length: 35 yards
To retain its full glaze we recommend that chintz be dry cleaned only.

Product Code *208* $16.50 per yard

Please note that all chintz swatches are shown at 25% of their actual size.

Chintz is made in the U.K.

Poppy
020113

Sapphire
020107

Rose
020114

Apricot
020116

Aquamarine
020340

Smoke
020106

Plum
020112

Buttermilk
020328

Jade
020339

Crimson
020317

Joy F125 Sand Multi White   *141139*

Hamilton F505 Terracotta Multi Cream   *092233*

Carousel F813 Mustard Multi Sapphire 383567

Chinoiserie F812 Kingfisher Multi Stone 382479

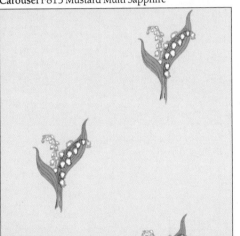

Lily of the Valley F487 Trop. Green Multi Stone 093508

Convolvulus L610 Multi Rose 060459

White Bower F364 Dark Green Multi Cream 195482

English Garden F367 Taupe Multi White 178486

Crystal F784 Crimson Multi White 381565

PLASTIC COATED FABRIC

In the tradition of Victorian oil cloth, Laura Ashley has developed a double thickness plastic-covered fabric suitable for tablecloths, indoor blinds and aprons.

This heavy plasticised country furnishing cotton, which may be easily cut, sewn and hemmed, is available in a selection of designs, including five new prints for 1986.

The fabric is not suitable for shower curtains.

Plastic Coated Fabric

Width: 115cm (45ins)
Maximum continuous length: 25 yards
Washing: do not wash or dry clean.
Wipe clean only with a damp cloth.

Product Code 205 $18.00 per yard

Made in the U.K. and the Netherlands.

74

Cherries F805 Black/White   374027

Emma C17 Multi Straw/Cream   517401

Rowan F686 Light Rose/Moss/White   365533

Nutmeg White/Burgundy   015084

Cornflowers F333 Sapphire Multi Mustard   187485

Dandelion F335 Terracotta/Moss/Cream   302270

Brighton Rock F389 Sugar Pink/White   174127

Marquee F556 Denim/White   334283

WALLPAPER & FABRIC BORDERS

Wallpaper and Fabric Borders are made in the U.K. and the Netherlands

WALLPAPER BORDERS

A border can soften the transition from wall to ceiling, while at dado level it provides a sense of proportion, harmonising with skirting and frieze.

A printed paper border can also be effective as an outline around a window, door or fireplace, perfectly defining the space and scale of any room.

Laura Ashley wallpaper borders are now available in forty-four different print/colourways, including ten new introductions, and two widths (110 mm and 55 mm) to co-ordinate with the wallpaper collection and other Home Furnishing products.

Wide borders 110 mm (4¼ ins), are shown on pages 76-77. Narrow borders, 55 mm (2¼ ins), are on pages 78-79.

Available in wallpaper borders.

Widths:
110 mm (4¼ ins) (one roll per pack)
55 mm (2¼ ins) (two rolls per pack)
Length per roll: 10 metres (11 yds)

Product Code 302 $7.00 per pack

FABRIC BORDERS

On covered furniture, curtains, blinds, pelmets, cushions or bedcovers, fabric borders make an attractive alternative to braid and fringing.

Laura Ashley fabric borders are available in a choice of thirty-one co-ordinated print/colourways, including nine new introductions, all in a plain weave pure cotton.

Wide borders 110 mm (4¼ ins) (plus a hem of 35-40 mm) are shown on pages 76-77. Narrow borders 55 mm (2¼ ins) (plus a hem of 35-40 mm) are shown on pages 78-79.

Available in fabric borders.

Widths: 110 mm (4¼ ins) or
              55 mm (2¼ ins)
Maximum continuous length: 20 metres
Washing: warm wash (40°C).
Medium hot iron.

Product Code 210
110 mm (4¼ ins) wide $4.50 per yard
55 mm (2¼ ins) wide $3.50 per yard

All borders are shown at 50% of actual size.

Bulrush F368 Terra.
Multi Cream 300233

Bulrush F368 Plum
Multi Cream 300504

Bulrush F368 Denim
Multi White 300506

Olive P897 Rose/Moss/White
063080

Olive P897 Sapphire/Moss/White
063088

Byron F539
White/Sand 344068

Byron F539
Sand/Dark Green 344280

Byron F539
Sand/Burgundy 344216

Byron F539 Cloud Blue/Oak
344282

Byron F539 Sand/Navy
344019

Juliet F7 Rose Multi White
068144

Clifford F391 Dark Silver Multi White
196483

Morning Parlour F591 Deep Sapphire Multi White
354497

Harbour F512 Kingfisher/Stone
346255

Harvest F116 Terracotta Multi Cream
151233

Rosy Swag
F627 Rose Multi White
355144

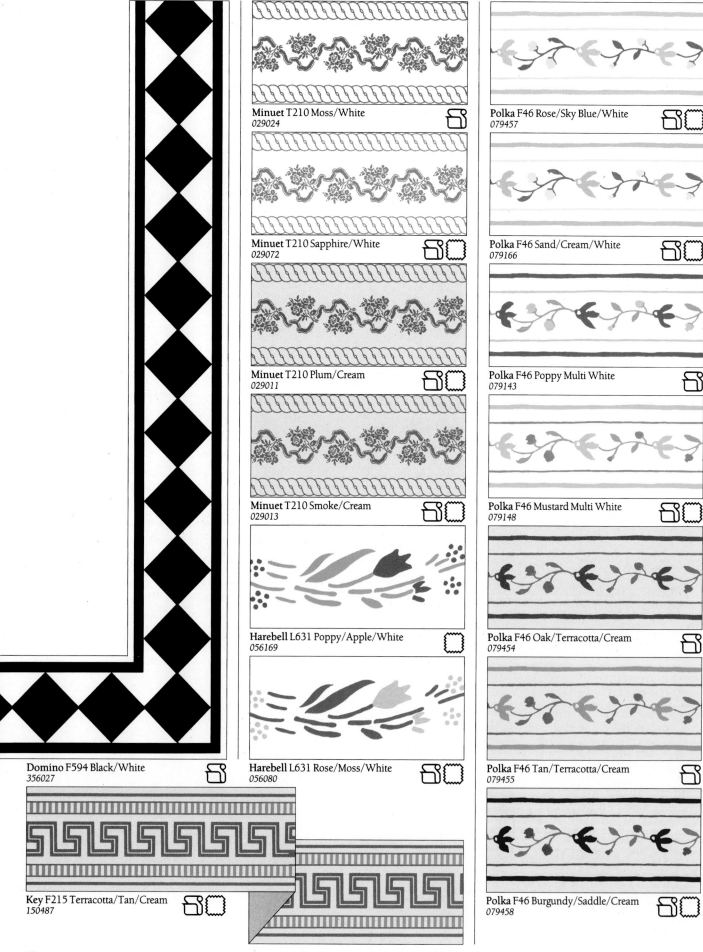

Domino F594 Black/White
356027

Key F215 Terracotta/Tan/Cream
150487

Minuet T210 Moss/White
029024

Minuet T210 Sapphire/White
029072

Minuet T210 Plum/Cream
029011

Minuet T210 Smoke/Cream
029013

Harebell L631 Poppy/Apple/White
056169

Harebell L631 Rose/Moss/White
056080

Polka F46 Rose/Sky Blue/White
079457

Polka F46 Sand/Cream/White
079166

Polka F46 Poppy Multi White
079143

Polka F46 Mustard Multi White
079148

Polka F46 Oak/Terracotta/Cream
079454

Polka F46 Tan/Terracotta/Cream
079455

Polka F46 Burgundy/Saddle/Cream
079458

Stratford F510 Rose Multi White
350144

Stratford F510 Aquamarine/Apricot/White
350268

Stratford F510 Smoke Multi Stone
350229

Stratford F510 Tan Multi Sand
350507

Trompe F762 Tan/Cream
377569

Trompe F762 Rose/White
377066

Trompe F762 Aquamarine/White
377206

Trompe F762 Sage/Cream
377032

Trompe F762 Burgundy/Sand
377217

Trompe F762 Apricot/White
377074

Trompe F762 Dark Green/Sand
377278

Trompe F762 Navy/Sand
377020

Swinburne F274 Burgundy/Navy/Sand *313260*

Trompe F762 Kingfisher/Stone
377255

TRIMMINGS

BIAS BINDING

A co-ordinating cotton binding in twenty-six colourways, including eight new introductions. Perfect for piping on cushions, loose covers and unfinished edges. Cut on the bias and folded into a hem for easier sewing, this 100% cotton binding, 2.5 cm (1 in) wide, is available by the yard.

Product Code 670 $1.50 per yard
Bias Binding is made in the U.K.

Cream	020110	Aquamarine	020340
Sand	020109	Mustard	020118
Straw	020329	Apple	020103
Sugar Pink	020327	Tropical Green	020299
Rose	020114	Poppy	020113
Guava	020330	Denim	020525
Terracotta	020111	Sapphire	020107
Apricot	020116	Moss	020102
Buttermilk	020328	Sage	020123
Jade	020339	Tan	020122
Crimson	020317	Dark Green	020101
Smoke	020106	Navy	020104
Plum	020112	Burgundy	020115

PLAIN GIMP

Available by the yard in a choice of eleven colourways, this 1.5 cm (⅝ in) wide gimp provides a simple but effective border on upholstery, chairs and lampshades. 100% viscose.

Product Code 719 $2.00 per yard

FRINGING

The ideal enhancement for any curtain, cushion or lampshade. Fringing in a choice of eleven co-ordinating colourways, including two new introductions, cream and crimson. 3.5 cm (1⅜ ins) wide.
Available by the yard. 100% viscose.

Product Code 718 $4.00 per yard

CORD TIE-BACKS

A neat, sophisticated finishing touch for any curtains or drapes – twisted cord tie-backs in eleven colourways. Each tie-back is finished with pommel ends and loop fittings. 55% cotton and 45% viscose.

Product Code 717 $22.00 per pair

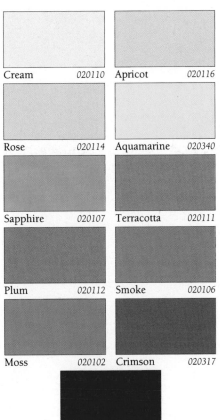

Cream	020110	Apricot	020116
Rose	020114	Aquamarine	020340
Sapphire	020107	Terracotta	020111
Plum	020112	Smoke	020106
Moss	020102	Crimson	020317
Burgundy	020115		

BRAID

A smart braid in a choice of nine colourways, woven exclusively for Laura Ashley from a hard-wearing mixture of 20% cotton, 80% viscose.

The braid, which is 1.5 cm (⅝ in) in width, is suitable for use on all upholstery, cushions and lampshades. Available by the yard.

Product Code 716 $3.50 per yard
Other trimmings are made in France.

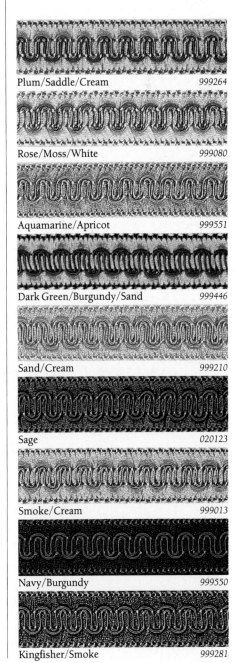

Plum/Saddle/Cream   999264

Rose/Moss/White   999080

Aquamarine/Apricot   999551

Dark Green/Burgundy/Sand   999446

Sand/Cream   999210

Sage   020123

Smoke/Cream   999013

Navy/Burgundy   999550

Kingfisher/Smoke   999281

Paint is made in the U.S.A.

PAINT

Think of a colour and imagine it on the walls of a room. Choose carefully and discover how its individual character can subtly create the atmosphere you want.

The coolness of jade; the warm glow of crimson; the classic understatement of buttermilk; or the softness of straw.

You might decide to add extra visual interest by dragging, washing or stippling, or simply by using a complementary gloss colour for woodwork and decorative detail. Or perhaps a printed paper border would better suit your taste. Whatever your preference, Laura Ashley flat and gloss paints provide the answer, in a range of eighteen flat and nineteen satin gloss colours, especially formulated to co-ordinate with Laura Ashley fabrics and wallpapers.

◀ FLAT PAINT

Laura Ashley latex matt flat paint (colours shown left) is produced with the most up-to-date polymers to give a durable matt finish for interiors.

Available in 2.5 litre (0.55 gallon) cans to cover 30 sq. metres (317 sq.feet).

Flat Paint	Product Code 401
2.5 litres	$24.00

SATIN GLOSS PAINT ▶

Laura Ashley satin gloss paint (colours shown right) is produced to a very high standard. Tough and dirt resistant for both interior and exterior use.

Available in 1 litre (1.76 pints) cans to cover 15 sq. metres (169 sq.feet).

Satin Gloss Paint	Product Code 402
1 litre	$16.50

For information on postal delivery charges on paint please contact Laura Ashley Mail Order Customer Services Department.

Flat Paint Colours

Colour	Code
White	020100
Stone	020300
Cream	020110
Pale Buttermilk	020331
Sand	020109
Soft Straw	020333
Soft Apricot	020293
Light Guava	020295
Light Terracotta	020294
Light Aquamarine	020290
Pale Jade	020332
Light Sage	020350
Soft Sapphire	020291
Light Smoke	020345
Light Kingfisher	020296
Soft Rose	020292
Light Plum	020347
Burgundy	020115

Satin Gloss Paint Colours

Colour	Code
White	020100
Stone	020300
Cream	020110
Buttermilk	020328
Sand	020109
Straw	020329
Apricot	020116
Terracotta	020111
Moss	020102
Jade	020339
Crimson	020317
Rose	020114
Plum	020112
Burgundy	020115
Smoke	020106
Kingfisher	020313
Navy	020104
Sapphire	020107
Poppy	020113

Ceramic Tiles are made in Italy.

CERAMIC TILES

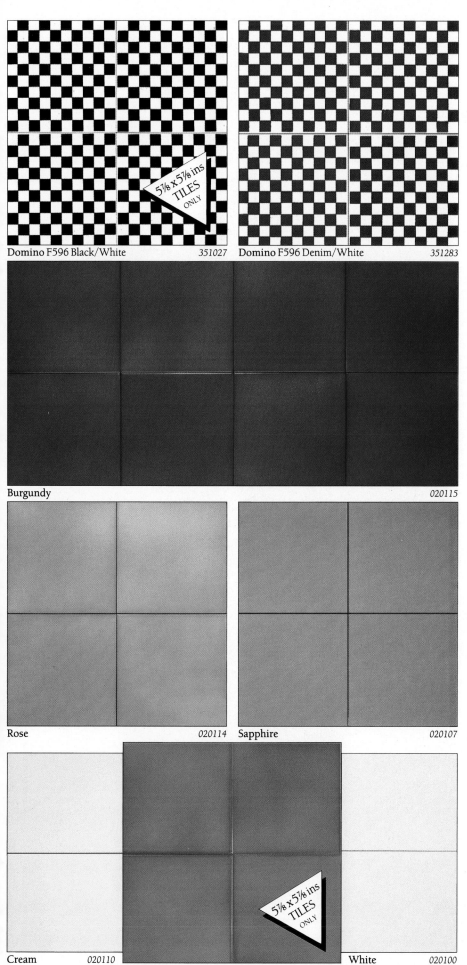

Domino F596 Black/White   *351027*

Domino F596 Denim/White   *351283*

Burgundy   *020115*

Rose   *020114*

Sapphire   *020107*

Cream   *020110*

Terracotta   *020111*

White   *020100*

Whether they might be found on a bathroom wall, a kitchen splash-back, or in a more formal room as a floor covering, tiles are an indispensable feature of any house.

Laura Ashley ceramic tiles are produced to a traditionally high quality, in a greater choice of print/colourways than ever before, including the new four colour Pavilion tile (see page 86), all with an easy to clean glazed ceramic surface.

FLOOR & WALL TILES

The large tiles, 20 x 20 cm (7⅞ x 7⅞ ins) in a choice of seventeen colourways, are particularly suitable for walls, and floors not subject to heavy wear. Professional advice may be required for application.

Available in packs of twenty-five to cover approximately one square metre (10 sq.feet).

Floor and Wall Tiles	Product Code *681*
Price per pack of 25	$87.50
Price per tile	$4.00

WALL TILES

The smaller tiles, 15 x 15 cm (5⅞ x 5⅞ ins) in a choice of twenty-one colourways, are easy to apply and should be used only on walls.

Available in packs of twenty-two to cover approximately half a square metre (5 sq. feet)

Wall Tiles	Product Code *686*
Price per pack of 22	$37.50
Price per tile	$2.00

For information on postal delivery charges on tiles and border tiles please contact Laura Ashley Mail Order Customer Services Department.

Pavilion F573 Poppy/Must./Apple/Denim *315558*

Wood Violet P753 Mustard/Apple/White *046194*

Bembridge F66 Burgundy/Navy/Sand *132260*

Pavilion F573 Black/White *315027*

7⅞ x 7⅞ ins TILES ONLY

Pavilion F573 Apricot/White *315116*

5⅞ x 5⅞ ins TILES ONLY

Pavilion F573 Rose/White *315066*

5⅞ x 5⅞ ins TILES ONLY

Cottage Sprig P767 Rose/Moss/White *053080*

Ming F132 China Blue/Sapphire/White *135162*

5⅞ x 5⅞ ins TILES ONLY

Trellis P768 Apple/White *054063*

7⅞ x 7⅞ ins TILES ONLY

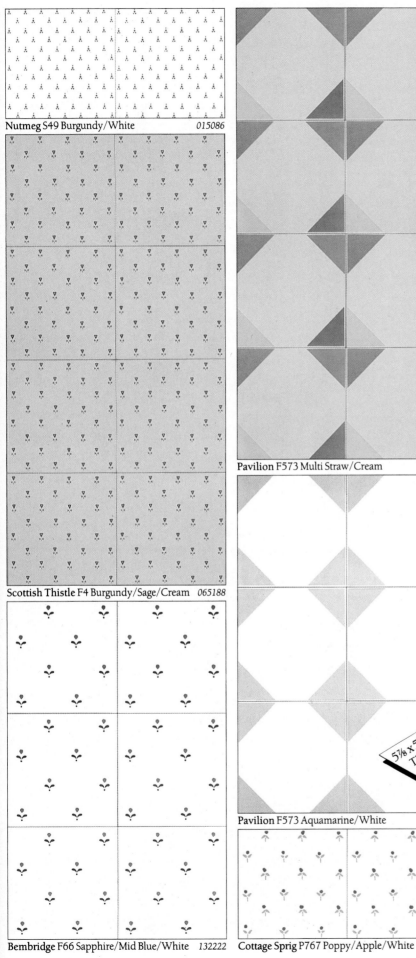

Nutmeg S49 Burgundy/White — 015086

Scottish Thistle F4 Burgundy/Sage/Cream — 065188

Bembridge F66 Sapphire/Mid Blue/White — 132222

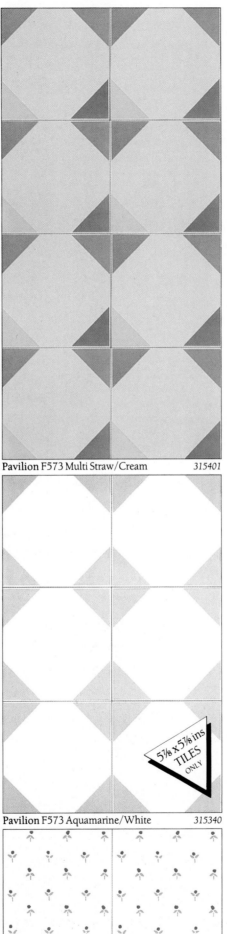

Pavilion F573 Multi Straw/Cream — 315401

5⅞ x 5⅞ ins TILES ONLY

Pavilion F573 Aquamarine/White — 315340

Cottage Sprig P767 Poppy/Apple/White — 053169

BORDER TILES

These small ceramic tiles are designed for use with the large 20 x 20 cm tiles, to provide an attractive finishing touch with a co-ordinating or contrasting border.

Border tiles measuring 10 x 20 cm (4 x 7⅞ ins) are available in a choice of six plain colours in packs of twenty-five to cover approximately half a square metre (5 sq.feet).

Product Code 688

Border Tiles
per pack of 25 $32.50

Border Tiles are made in Italy.

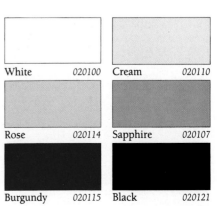

White	020100	Cream	020110
Rose	020114	Sapphire	020107
Burgundy	020115	Black	020121

Fabric Pleated Shades left to right: **Wild Clematis** Smoke/Cream, **Petite Fleur** Cream/Smoke & **Emma** Multi Straw/Cream   Ceramic Lampbases: **Crackle-glaze Cream**

LAURA ASHLEY LIGHTING

Once the overall decoration of a room is complete, stand back and devote some thought as to how it can best be shown. Here lighting is all important. If not given sufficient consideration, incorrect lighting can totally alter the look of a room through inappropriate style or colour.

Since the invention of the electric light, Oriental jars and vases have provided the inspiration for decorative lampbases. Our classic ginger jar bases paired with our broad array of patterned fabric and pleated empire shape lampshades offer the perfect co-ordinate to your English-inspired interiors.

Each ceramic base is available in three sizes – with a choice of clear kiln-fired glaze or in our new double-fired authentic crackle glaze. These classic bases can be combined with any of our 20 Laura Ashley patterned fabric shades to complete your room's co-ordination.

Classic ceramic ginger jar bases shown below, in clear white glaze (also available in clear cream glaze). Each fabric pleated lampshade is available in three sizes to fit each base perfectly.

Our new crackle glaze ceramic ginger jar lampbases shown on the left in cream crackle glaze (also available in white crackle glaze) with three of our patterned fabric pleated lampshades.

Each of our fabric pleated lampshades is available in small, medium, and large sizes (to fit perfectly in proportion our ginger jar lampbases) and is available in a choice of 20 of our newest and most popular fabric prints and colours (shown overleaf).

Fabric Pleated Shades left to right: Rose, Cornflowers Sapphire Multi Mustard & Imogen Cherry Multi White   Ceramic Lampbases: **White**

FABRIC PLEATED
LAMPSHADES

Large Lampshade
Height: 11½ ins, diameter: 16 ins
Product Code 576 $36.00

Medium Lampshade
Height: 11½ ins, diameter: 14 ins
Product Code 577 $31.00

Small Lampshade
Height 7½ ins, diameter: 10 ins
Product Code 578 $26.00

CERAMIC LAMPBASES

Large Rounded Lampbase
Ht. from base to top of lamp: 24¾ ins
Clear-glaze
Product Code 573 $42.50
Crackle-glaze
Product Code 579 $44.50

Medium Rounded Lampbase
Ht. from base to top of lamp: 21¼ ins
Clear-glaze
Product Code 574 $36.50
Crackle-glaze
Product Code 572 $38.50

Small Rounded Lampbase
Ht. from base to top of clip shade: 14½ ins
Clear-glaze
Product Code 575 $32.50
Crackle-glaze
Product Code 594 $34.50

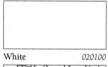

White   020100   Cream   020110

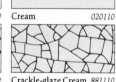

Crackle-glaze White 881100   Crackle-glaze Cream 881110

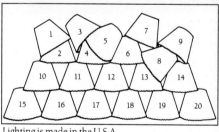

No.	Pattern	Code
1	Nutmeg S49 Cream Plum	015012
2	Nutmeg S49 Sand/Navy	015019
3	Floribunda L577 Multi Apricot	042096
4	Polly F511 Cherry Multi White	322244
5	Fretwork F772 Multi Buttermilk	376409
6	Petite Fleur R150 Cream/Smoke	026014
7	Palmetto F303 Aquamarine/Apricot/White	184268
8	Kate F373 Rose/Moss/White	173080
9	Cornflowers F333 Sapphire Multi Mustard	187485
10	Paisley F477 Smoke/Kingfisher/Cream	332500
11	Campion R143 White/Rose	021067
12	Kate F373 Sapphire/Apple/White	173190
13	Rose	020114
14	Wild Clematis S65 Smoke/Cream	004013
15	Fretwork F772 Multi Smoke	376417
16	Wild Clematis S65 Cream/Plum	004012
17	Paisley F477 Burgundy/Navy/Tan	332555
18	Imogen F471 Cherry Multi White	097244
19	Emma C17 Multi Straw/Cream	517401
20	Penelope F535 Mint Multi White	095396

Lighting is made in the U.S.A.

COLUMN LAMPBASE
& SHADE

Our solid wood turned lampbase adapts the age old candlestick silhouette for modern day electric lighting. Each base is hand-accented with bands of decorative colour that is picked up again on the solid colour lampshade.

These charming lampbases and shades are available in five colour combinations for 1986:

Burgundy on sand lampbase with solid burgundy lampshade.
Apricot on white lampbase with solid apricot lampshade.
Sapphire on white lampbase with solid sapphire lampshade.
Aquamarine on white lampbase with solid aquamarine lampshade.
Rose on white lampbase with solid rose lampshade.

Column Lampbase and Shade
Product Code 570 $50.00

Shown below from left to right

Burgundy Shade & Sand Column Lampbase	0217
Apricot Shade & White Column Lampbase	0074
Sapphire Shade & White Column Lampbase	0072
Aquamarine Shade & White Column Lampbase	0206
Rose Shade & White Column Lampbase	0066

The Dining Collection is made in the U.K.

DINING COLLECTION

At breakfast, lunch, tea or dinner, a tablecloth provides a civilised finishing touch for kitchen or dining room.

The perfect background for any occasion, Laura Ashley printed tablecloths, with napkins, place-mats and dining accessories, are produced in an easy to co-ordinate range of prints and colours.

There is no reason to confine a tablecloth to the dining room. Throw a round tablecloth over a simple chipboard table to create an instant draped table, smart enough for the most elegant drawing room or bedroom.

Laura Ashley tablecloths are available in four sizes, all with neat, bound, scalloped edges. Each size is available in six print/colourways.

Small Round Tablecloth
178 cm (70 ins) diameter
Product Code 499 $32.00
Large Round Tablecloth
228 cm (90 ins) diameter
Product Code 498 $42.00
Square Tablecloth
132 x 132 cm (52 x 52 ins)
Product Code 497 $22.00
Rectangular Tablecloth
132 x 178 cm (52 x 70 ins)
Product Code 496 $32.00

Co-ordinating quilted place-mats, tea-cosies, egg-cosies and oven gloves, together with aprons and napkins are also available, in a choice of six print/colourways.

Place-mat 30 x 45 cm (12 x 17¾ ins)
Product Code 524 $8.00
Tea-cosy 36.5 x 26 cm (14½ x 10 ins)
Product Code 522 $16.50
Egg-cosy 11.5 x 13 cm (4½ x 5 ins)
Product Code 523 $5.00
Set of four napkins 42 cm (16½ ins) sq.
Product Code 503 $16.00
Apron   Each $4.00
Product Code 531 $19.50
Oven gloves
Product Code 495 $19.00

All dining collection table linen is printed with specially formulated dyes, particularly suited to items subject to frequent washing. Quilted items should be washed at 40°C. Cool iron.

KEY TO PHOTOGRAPHS

TABLECLOTHS
1. **Emma** C17 Multi Straw/Cream *517401*
2. **Cottage Sprig** P767 Rose/Moss/White *053080*
3. **Morning Parlour**
   F474 Deep Sapphire Multi White *098497*
4. **Dandelion**
   F335 Denim/Tropical Green/White *302448*
5. **Mr. Jones** F381 Navy/Burgundy/Sand *190261*
6. **Dandelion**
   F335 Terracotta/Moss/Cream *302270*

PLACE-MATS, TEA-COSIES, EGG-COSIES NAPKINS, APRONS & OVEN GLOVES
1. **Studio** F792 Multi Straw/Cream *370401*
2. **Cottage Sprig** P767 Rose/Moss/Wh. *053080*
3. **Polly** F511 Cherry Multi White *322244*
4. **Marquee** F556 Denim/White *334283*
5. **Nutmeg** S49 Sand/Navy *015019*
6. **Milfoil** L570 Cream/Terracotta *040030*

HARD MATS & TRAYS

A new collection of fine dining accessories. Large serving mats, place-mats and coasters in a choice of two prints: Sophie and Mr. Jones. The mats are finished in cellulose and have a soft green felt reverse to prevent scratches.

This useful new range is completed by a sturdy wooden tray in a choice of two prints, to co-ordinate with Sophie and Mr. Jones, finished with melamine, a smart gold edge and green felt reverse.

Tray
54 x 39 cm (21 x 15 ins)
Product Code 726 $75.00

Large Place-Mats
25 x 35 cm (10 x 14 ins)
Product Code 534   Box of 2 $25.00

Small Place-Mats
20 x 24 cm (8 x 9½ ins)
Product Code 532   Box of 6 $63.00
Coasters   Each $10.50
9 x 11 cm (3½ x 4¼ ins)
Product Code 533   Box of 6 $19.00

▲ Small and Large Place-Mats & Coasters   Sophie F614 Multi Straw/Cream *352401*
▲ Tray   Emma C17 Multi Straw/Cream *517401*
▼ Small and Large Place-Mats, Coasters & Tray   Mr. Jones F381 Navy/Burgundy/Sand *190261*

Hard Mats and Trays are made in the U.K.

CRAFTS

PATCHWORK PIECES

Patchwork pieces with easy to follow instructions, in a selection of colour co-ordinated packs.

Square patchwork pieces are available in packs of approximately 100 pieces, 12 cm (4¾ ins) sq. to cover a minimum area of one sq. metre (10 sq. feet).

Square Patchwork Pieces
Product Code 674 $10.00 per pack

Hexagonal patchwork pieces are available in packs of approximately 120 pieces, 10 cm (4 ins) across to cover a minimum area of one sq. metre (10 sq. feet).

Hexagonal Patchwork Pieces
Product Code 680 $10.00 per pack

Sapphire 020107	Poppy 020113	Rose 020114
Plum 020112	Burgundy/ Navy 020550	Apricot 020116
Kingfisher 020313	Smoke 020106	Moss 020102	Terracotta 020111

TAPESTRY CUSHION KIT

This simple, easy to sew kit enables you to recreate a choice of four designs.

Contents: No.16 100% white mono canvas 50 cm (20 ins) sq., tapestry needle, 100% wool Paterna Persian Yarn to complete a design of approximately 35 cm (13¾ ins) sq., instructions and a stitch diagram.

1. Kew Gardens F484 Mint Multi White	090396
2. Blue Ribbons F200 Smoke Multi Stone	140229
3. Morning Parlour F474 Deep Sapph. Multi Wh.	098497
4. Grapes F62 Smoke Multi Cream	158247

Tapestry Cushion Kit
Product Code 500 $45.00

TAPESTRY PIN CUSHION KIT

Recreate the Laura Ashley design Kate on a pin cushion.

Contents: No.16 100% white mono canvas 25 cm (10 ins) sq., tapestry needle, 100% wool Paterna Persian Yarn to complete a design of approximately 14 cm (5½ ins) sq., instructions and a stitch diagram.

Tapestry Pin Cushion Kit
Product Code 528
Reference No. 173080 $19.00

Patchwork pieces are made in the U.K. and the Netherlands. Other Crafts are made in the U.K.

CUSHIONS

FRILLED & FLAT BORDERED CUSHION COVERS

This year the range of frilled cushion covers has been extended to incorporate several new designs and a new flat bordered cover in a choice of three plain colourways, with a wide printed border edging. Covers, in pure cotton, may be purchased either separately, or with soft feather cushion pads of the highest quality.

Round Frilled Cushion Cover*
34 cm (13½ ins) diameter (incl. frill)
Product Code *513* $25.00

Square Frilled Cushion Cover*
50 x 50 cm (19¾ x 19¾ ins) (incl. frill)
Product Code *512* $25.00

Flat Bordered Cushion Cover*
50 x 50 cm (19¾ x 19¾ ins)
Product Code *526* $25.00

Round Pad
Product Code *519* $12.00

Square Pad
Product Code *518* $12.00

*Pads not included.

1	Flat Bordered Cushion	
	Burgundy with **Stratford** Border	020115
2	Square Frilled Cushion	
	Mr. Jones Navy/Burgundy/Sand	190261
3	Round Frilled Cushion	
	Paisley Plum/Saddle/Cream	332264
4	Round Frilled Cushion	
	Dandelion Terracotta/Moss/Cream	302270
5	Square Frilled Cushion	
	Cricket Stripe Terracotta/Moss/Cream	185449
6	Sq. Frilled Cushion **Riviera** Sapphire/Mustard	131221
7	Round Frilled Cushion	
	Cornflowers Sapphire Multi Mustard	187485
8	Rnd. Frilled Cushion **Penelope** Mint Multi Wh.	095396
9	Round Frilled Cushion **Kate** Rose/Moss/White	173080
10	Square Frilled Cushion	
	Kew Gardens Mint Multi White	090396
11	Flat Bordered Cush. **Rose** with **Stratford** Border	020114
12	Round Frilled Cushion	
	Regency Stripe Apricot/Aquamarine/White	197265
13	Round Frilled Cushion	
	Paisley Smoke/Kingfisher/Cream	332500
14	Square Frilled Cushion	
	Regency Stripe Aquamarine/Apricot/White	197268
15	Flat Bordered Cushion	
	Smoke with **Stratford** Border	020106
16	Square Frilled Cushion	
	Palmetto Kingfisher/Burgundy/Cream	184256
17	Square Frilled Cushion **Campion** White/Rose	021067
18	Rnd Frilled Cushion **Kate** Sapphire/Apple/Wh.	173190

Cushions are made in the U.K.

CUSHIONS

PIPED CUSHION COVERS

Piped square cushion covers are now available in two colourways of the new Grand Paisley print, and one of the co-ordinating small Paisley print. This year also sees the introduction of three new piped chintz cushions, to give eight plain colourways in chintz, as well as the new White Bower cushion.

The Emma print is also available as a piped square cushion cover, in country furnishing cotton with a plain rose piping.

New to this year's collection is a piped appliqué cushion in two colourways, incorporating a fabric border on a plain square of country furnishing cotton.

Square Piped Cushion Cover 40 x 40 cm (15½ x 15½ ins) Product Code *511*	**$22.00**
Square Piped Chintz Cushion Cover 40 x 40 cm (15½ x 15½ ins) Product Code *525*	**$22.00**
Appliqué Cushion Cover 40 x 40 cm (15½ x 15½ ins) Product Code *527*	**$23.50**
Square Pad Product Code *518*	**$12.00**

No.	Description	Code
1	Square Piped Cushion	
	Paisley Burgundy/Navy/Tan	*332555*
2	Square Piped Cushion	
	Grand Paisley Multi Burgundy	*363243*
3	Sq. Piped Cushion **Grand Paisley** Multi Navy	*363413*
4	Square Piped Chintz Cushion	
	White Bower Dark Green Multi Cream	*195482*
5	Square Piped Chintz Cushion **Poppy**	*020113*
6	Square Piped Chintz Cushion **Sapphire**	*020107*
7	Square Piped Chintz Cushion **Plum**	*020112*
8	Appliqué Cushion **Plum** with **Minuet** Border	*020112*
9	Square Piped Chintz Cushion **Aquamarine**	*020340*
10	Square Piped Chintz Cushion **Smoke**	*020106*
11	Square Piped Chintz Cushion **Jade**	*020339*
12	Appliqué Cushion **Sapphire** with **Polka** Border	*020107*
13	Sq. Piped Cushion **Emma** Multi Straw/Cream	*517401*
14	Square Piped Chintz Cushion **Apricot**	*020116*
15	Square Piped Chintz Cushion **Rose**	*020114*

Patchwork Quilts are made in the U.K.

PATCHWORK QUILTS

Laura Ashley patchwork quilts, handmade in Wales in two traditional designs using Laura Ashley fabrics, co-ordinate easily with the entire bedlinen collection. The quilts, designed to fit easily over standard single and double beds, are available in two distinctive styles—Mosaic, in a choice of rose and aquamarine combination or apricot and aquamarine, and Lattice in five colourways: rose, plum, sapphire, smoke and apricot.

Single Mosaic Patchwork Quilt
1.5 x 2.5 metres (59 x 98 ins)
Product Code 678 $195.00

Double Mosaic Patchwork Quilt
2.4 x 2.5 metres (94 x 98 ins)
Product Code 678 $295.00

Single Lattice Patchwork Quilt
1.5 x 2.5 metres (59 x 98 ins)
Product Code 679 $225.00

Double Lattice Patchwork Quilt
2.4 x 2.5 metres (94 x 98 ins)
Product Code 679 $350.00

Dry clean only. Cool iron to retain the fullness of the quilted fibre filling.

1.	Sapphire Lattice Patchwork Quilt	
	Single 920107	Double 921107
2.	Smoke Lattice Patchwork Quilt	
	Single 920106	Double 921106
3.	Plum Lattice Patchwork Quilt	
	Single 920112	Double 921112
4.	Rose Lattice Patchwork Quilt	
	Single 920114	Double 921114
5.	Apricot Lattice Patchwork Quilt	
	Single 920116	Double 921116
6.	Rose/Aquamarine Mosaic Patchwork Quilt	
	Single 920556	Double 921556
7.	Apricot/Aquamarine Mosaic Patchwork Quilt	
	Single 920552	Double 921552

LAURA ASHLEY LACE

That lace has been highly prized since the seventeenth century is evident from its appearance in so many master-pieces of portraiture in art galleries the world over. Today this most intricate of crafts is still alive in England.

Laura Ashley Nottingham lace panels, tablecloths and bedspreads are produced on original nineteenth century Jacquard-looms in delicate designs of floral swags and arabesques.

All lace is hand or machine washable (40°C). Cool iron.

LACE PANELS

With or without curtains, lace panels make an attractive window screen.

Each panel has an open hem at the top for easy hanging.

Lace Panel
152 x 228 cm (60 x 90 ins)
Available in white or ivory.
Product Code 773 $55.00 each

LACE TABLECLOTH

A tablecloth to give any table an air of Victorian elegance.

Lace Tablecloth
178 x 224 cm (70 x 88 ins)
Available in white or ivory.
Product Code 530 $75.00

LACE BY THE YARD

In a similar design to the lace panel.
Width: 152cm (60 ins) Available in white or ivory. Product Code 229
8 pt. lace $15.00 per yard
12 pt. lace $20.00 per yard

White	020100	Ivory	020763

LACE BEDSPREADS

Give a bedroom an atmosphere of romance with a delicate lace bedspread.

Single Lace Bedspread
188 x 264 cm (74 x 104 ins)
Product Code 529
White   Reference No. 920100 $100.00
Ivory   Reference No. 920763 $100.00

Double Lace Bedspread
254 x 279 cm (100 x 110 ins)
Product Code 529
White   Reference No. 921100 $125.00
Ivory   Reference No. 921763 $125.00

TEA FOR TWO SET

Perfect for tea or coffee, this fine bone-china, decorated with the Cottage Sprig design in rose and moss, includes two cups and saucers, two plates, creamer, sugar bowl and teapot.

Product Code 682
Reference No. 053080 $75.00

Lace and Tea for Two Set are made in the U.K.

LAURA ASHLEY BEDLINENS

Begin your bedroom's decoration most naturally with the bed. Here for you is the Laura Ashley collection of bedlinens for 1986. Designed by Mrs. Ashley for Burlington Mills of easy-care 200 count cale, a blend of 50% pure cotton and 50% Celanese Fortrel polyester. Each ensemble co-ordinates perfectly with Mrs. Ashley's renowned collection of wallcoverings, fabrics by-the-yard, and decorative accessories.

PENELOPE

Charming rose coloured buds on a mint green dotted background creates a fresh-from-the-garden ambience for our new Penelope pattern. A soft white hem attached with mint green border finishes off the sheets and pillow cases. The Penelope pattern, forms the background for Kew Gardens, a larger botanical print of varying flowers that appears on one side of the quilted comforter, the pillow shams and the headroll.

Prices are shown on page 106.

PAISLEY

Age-old English fascination
with the East brings us this
handsome bedlinen pattern
- Paisley - formed of neat
swirls of smoke and kingfisher
blue on a ground of soft
cream and finished with a
cream border attached with
kingfisher piping.
The comforter reverses to
solid smoke blue.

Prices are shown on page 106.

HARRIET

Small budding blossoms of cherry and old lavender on a random bed of pointillist dots form the inspiration for this bedlinen pattern. A soft white hem attached with old lavender piping finishes the basic sheets and pillow cases. The quilted comforter reverses to Imogen, a print of tiny blossoms and vines in the same colorations and also covers the headroll. All other accessories are in the Harriet sheeting pattern.

Prices are shown on page 106.

CASTLEBERRY

Shown above. Primitive stencil patterns of tulips form the design inspiration for this, our most classic Laura Ashley bedlinen pattern, Harebell. Cottage Sprig, in rose and moss green on white is used throughout the complementary small floral of the sheets and accessories bordered with a larger stencil vine of the same colours. The comforter reverses to the large stencil vine stripe and is repeated on the flounced pillow shams and headroll. Prices are shown below.

PALMETTO

Shown right. This cool and inviting pattern of palms in aquamarine and apricot on soft white is bordered with a soft white hem and apricot piping. The comforter reverses to our charming Regency Stripe of the same colours that is also used for the co-ordinating pillow shams and headroll. Prices are shown below.

BURLINGTON PATTERNED BEDLINEN PRICE LIST

Sheets Flat or Fitted

Twin	$24.00
Full	$32.00
Queen	$38.00
King	$45.00
California King	$45.00

Pillow Cases (per pair)

Standard	$30.00
King	$33.00

Sham - Standard	$40.00	
	King	$48.00

Duvet Covers*

Twin	$80.00
Full	$90.00
Queen	$105.00
King	$115.00

* Duvet Covers available in Castleberry only

Dust Ruffle
A full ruffled skirt that completes each design.

Twin	$65.00
Full	$75.00
Queen	$85.00
King	$95.00
California King	$95.00

Comforter Quilted and filled with 100% Celanese Fortrel polyester.

Twin	$130.00
Full	$155.00
Queen	$185.00
King	$222.00

Shower Curtain* $50.00
* Bembridge, Paisley or Harriet

Pillows

Sq. Decorative	$35.00
Rd. Decorative*	$35.00

* Bembridge or Palmetto only

Breakfast Square* $35.00
* Available in Penelope, Harriet and Paisley only

Decorative Pillow* $35.00
* Pillows are not available in Castleberry

BEMBRIDGE

Shown above. Bembridge, our stencil design in flowers of sapphire and china blues on a soft white forms the design of this charming bedlinen pattern. A self-patterned hem bordered with our china blue Cricket Stripe carries throughout the sheets, pillow cases and pillow shams. The comforter reverses to our crisp blue on white stripe and is used again on the decorative pillows. Prices are shown on page 106.

TICKING STRIPE

Shown left. Classic ticking stripes in rose on a fresh white ground hemmed with a flounce and rose piping create one of our most popular bedlinen designs. The comforter reverses to Rosamund, rose buds with green leaves on white. Prices are shown below.

BURLINGTON TICKING STRIPE PRICE LIST

Fitted Sheets		Flat Sheets		Sham		Comforter		Dust Ruffle	
						Quilted and filled with 100% Celanese Fortrel Polyester.		A full ruffled skirt that completes each line design.	
Twin	$19.00	Twin	$19.00	Standard	$36.00				
Full	$25.00	Full	$25.00	King	$42.00				
Queen	$34.00	Queen	$34.00	Duvet Covers				Twin	$60.00
King	$40.00	King	$40.00	Twin	$70.00	Twin	$100.00	Full	$70.00
California King	$40.00	Pillows Cases (per pair)		Full	$80.00	Full	$120.00	Queen	$80.00
		Standard	$25.00	Queen	$95.00	Queen	$150.00	King	$90.00
		King	$28.00	King	$110.00	King	$175.00	California King	$90.00

All Laura Ashley Bedlinen is made in the U.S.A.

DRESSING ROOM COLLECTION

Beauty of design and purity of function combine naturally in our Laura Ashley Dressing Room Collection.

SPONGE BAG/COSMETIC BAGS

Each lined in white plastic with an interior pocket and zippered closing.

Sm. Cosmetic Bag 6½ x 1¼ x 4½ins high
Product Code 563 $8.50
Cosmetic Bag 8¼ x 2⅛ x 5¼ins high
Product Code 564 $12.50
Sponge Bag 12 x 4¼ x 9ins high
Product Code 565 $16.50

SEWING OR JEWELRY BOX

Featuring two large interior compartments with a removable tray.

12 x 8 x 3ins high
Product Code 567 $30.00

TISSUE BOX COVER

Slip our attractive cover over your standard tissue box.

10½ x 4¾ x 3⅜ins high
Product Code 569 $10.50

SEWING KIT

A handy kit with useful pins, needles, tape measure, and a plait of threads.

5¾ x 9⅛ins opened
Product Code 535 $12.50

ROUND PIN CUSHION
SEWING BOX

Filled with a multi-coloured plait of threads, tape measure, pins and needles.

4 x 4 x 3⅜ins high
Product Code 557 $16.00

PICTURE FRAMES

Padded frames in the same print/colourways as our Dressing Room Collection.

Medium Single Picture Frame
5 x 6½ins (holds 3½ x 5ins photo)
Product Code 541 $13.50

Large Single Picture Frame
7 x 9ins (holds 5 x 7ins photo)
Product Code 542 $16.50

Small Square Picture Frame
5 x 5ins (holds a 3½ x 3½ins photo)
Product Code 543 $11.50

Double Folding Frame with oval mats
5 x 6½ins (holds two 3½ x 5ins photos)
Product Code 544 $16.00

▲ Dressing Room Collection & Photograph Frames   Kate F373 Rose/Moss/White *173080*
▼ Dressing Room Collection   Regatta B10 Sapphire/White *086072*

Paisley F477
Smoke/Kingfisher/Cream   *332500*

Emma C17
Multi Straw/Cream   *517401*

Palmetto F303
Aquamarine/Apricot/White *184268*

Paisley F477
Plum/Saddle/Cream   *332264*

Cornflowers F333
Sapphire Multi Mustard   *187485*

Brighton Rock F389
Sugar Pink/White   *174127*

DESK COLLECTION

▲ Desk Collection & Photograph Frames
▼ Desk Collection & Photograph Frames

Penelope F535 Mint Multi White *095396*
Cornflowers F333 Sapphire Multi Mustard *187485*

Palmetto F303
Aquamarine/Apricot/White *184268*

Paisley F477
Plum/Saddle/Cream *332264*

Simla F516
Multi Allspice *331399*

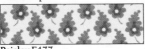

Paisley F477
Smoke/Kingfisher/Cream *332500*

Kate F373
Rose/Moss/White *173080*

* Not available in all prints, please call Mail Order for specific colours.
Dressing Room Collection made in U.S.A. and U.K.

A collection of fabric-covered writing accessories in a choice of seven prints. Perfect for sitting room, study or bedroom.

PHOTOGRAPH ALBUM

A cloth-bound, expanding album with 10 clear vinyl self-adhesive pages.
Photograph Album
Product Code 553 $35.00

Pack of 10 Pages for Photograph Album
Product Code 554 $8.00 per pack

COLLECTOR'S ALBUM

Perfect for scraps, momentoes, pressed flowers, or what you will.
* Product Code 550 $35.00

FOLDER

Fabric-covered, with deep side pocket and plain writing pad (11¾ x 8¼ ins).
Product Code 546 $25.00

DESK BLOTTER

Plain fabric trim and green felt reverse.
* Product Code 556 $17.50

1986 DESK DIARY

With a plain, cloth-bound spine. One week to a view. A ring binder system allows you to insert your own information sheets, and replace the diary pages year by year. Refills available.
* Diary — Product Code 547 $22.50
   Refill — Product Code 547 $13.50

POCKET DIARY

* Product Code 540 $8.00

DESK PAD

Desk Pad
Product Code 545 $12.00

Desk Pad Refills
Product Code 593 $5.00

ADDRESS BOOK

* Product Code 549 $14.50

NOTEBOOK

* Product Code 876 $10.00

WASTEPAPER BASKET

Paper-covered, folding basket.
* Product Code 555 $24.50

TOWELS
BY BURLINGTON

A new range of solid and printed bath towels, hand towels, wash cloths, bath sheets and bath mats.

LAURA ASHLEY
SOLID COLOURED TOWELS

In extra large and extra thirsty 100% cotton in 10 classic Laura Ashley colours. Each colour is available as a bath towel, bath sheet, hand towel, and wash cloth. Colours from top to bottom are: old lavender (draped), navy, smoke, sapphire, plum, rose, apricot, aquamarine, cream and white.

Bath Towel 28 x 52 ins
Product Code 622 $15.00

Hand Towel 17 x 30 ins
Product Code 623 $9.00

Wash Cloth 13 x 13 ins
Product Code 624 $4.00

Bath Sheet 36 x 70 ins
Product Code 882 $27.00

Rose 020114	White 020100	Aquamarine 020340
Sapphire 020107	Plum 020112	Navy 020104	Smoke 020106
Apricot 020116	Old Lavender 020352	Cream 020110

LAURA ASHLEY
PRINTED TOWELS

Our 100% cotton terry-looped towels with just a touch of polyester for durability, in three of our most popular patterns, each with a contrasting piping on the hem.

Bembridge – floral design in sapphire and mid-blue on a white ground with sapphire piping.
Paisley – smoke and kingfisher swirls on a soft cream ground with smoke piping.
Harriet – blossoms of cherry and old lavender with green leaves on a white ground, with old lavender piping.

Bath Towel 25 x 50 ins
Product Code 622 $17.00

Hand Towel 16 x 30 ins
Product Code 623 $11.00

Wash Cloth 13 x 13 ins
Product Code 624 $5.00

Bath Mat 22 x 34 ins
Product Code 881 $18.00

All towels are made in the U.S.A.

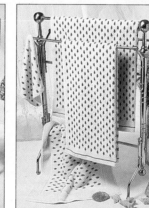
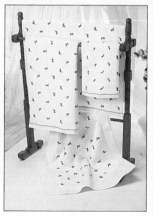

Bembridge F66
Sapphire/Mid Blue/White   *132222*

Paisley F477
Smoke/Kingfisher/Cream   *332500*

Harriet F473
F473 Cherry/Multi White   *096244*

MADE TO MEASURE & FURNITURE SERVICES

MADE TO MEASURE
CURTAINS

Add a professional touch to any interior with Laura Ashley's exclusive Made to Measure service in curtains, pelmets and blinds. Our many years of experience in interior design and the intricacies of sewing combine with first class workmanship and quality control to produce a high standard in every aspect of these services.

Plain or frilled, in country furnishing cotton, chintz or drawing room fabric, and fully lined in white or cream satinised lining fabric, every pair of Laura Ashley curtains is expertly finished to the customer's specific requirements. The wide choice of prints and colourways ensures easy co-ordination with existing decoration.

Every pair of curtains is individually hand-finished to maintain a personal character, along with a high standard of expert craftsmanship.

PLAIN CURTAINS

The 7 cm (2¾ ins) deep, pencil-pleated heading tape has three alternative pockets, allowing the curtains to be fitted extremely close to the ceiling if so required. Each hem is separately turned to a depth of 6 cm (2½ ins).

▲ Plain Curtains, Pelmet & Tie-backs in **Chinoiserie** Kingfisher Multi Stone

▼ Pencil Pleats

▼ Hem and Lining Fabric

Frilled Curtains, Pelmet & Tie-backs in **Crystal Crimson Multi White**

Tie-back

▼ Lining Fabric and Heading tape

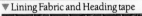

MADE TO MEASURE
CURTAINS

FRILLED CURTAINS

Frilled curtains have a 9 cm (3½ ins) wide, double-sided frill sewn on to the leading edge to give a delightfully feminine look.

When in striped fabric, the stripe of the frill itself will be perpendicular to the stripe of the curtain.

TIE - BACKS

Pairs of bound tie-backs are available to co-ordinate with the curtains. Stiffened and piped in a plain fabric they give any curtain a smart appearance.

PELMETS

As a decorative effect, to cover the top of a curtain, hiding the track and disguising window proportions, Laura Ashley presents a new pelmet service in two styles.

The gathered pelmet with a 9 cm (3½ ins) deep frill, produces a delightfully countrified look, while a plain gathered pelmet with a simple binding creates a classic tailored effect. All Laura Ashley pelmets are lined in either white or cream satinised lining fabric and have a single pocket heading tape 3 cm (1¼ ins) below the top of the pelmet.

Recommendations on the correct proportion of pelmet to curtain length are provided on page 171.

Ordering: curtains and pelmets may be ordered in any of the prints and colourways currently offered in country furnishing cotton, chintz or drawing room fabric.

For details of how to order see page 171.

BLINDS

FESTOON BLINDS ▶

Many an early nineteenth century house would have presented a perfect example of the elegance of the festoon blind. In reality a type of frilled curtain reefed up on cords to hang in flamboyant swags, let down at night.

By day graceful cascades of cloth hang at regular intervals over the upper part of the window in a contrast to the lines of woodwork and curtains, giving any room an atmosphere of tranquility.

These frilled blinds are available in country furnishing cotton, chintz and drawing room fabric.

Each blind is weighted, fully lined in white or cream satinised lining fabric, and has a 2¾ ins. deep pencil-pleat heading and 3½ ins. deep piped frill sewn into the bottom edge.

Fittings supplied with the blinds – head rails, brackets, hooks and gliders – are manufactured for Laura Ashley using high grade nylon and precision engineered aluminium. The simple raising mechanism is operated by a fine cord with a brass pull, while an advanced ratchet system allows the blind to be secured at any level.

See page 171 for ordering details.

ROMAN BLINDS ▶

The classic Roman blind fits neatly into the exact area of the window. Fully lined in white or cream satinised lining fabric, the blinds are easily detached from the rail to make cleaning as simple as possible. Fittings supplied with the blinds: head rails and brackets are made from high grade nylon and precision engineered aluminium. The simple raising mechanism is operated by a fine cord with a brass pull, while the same successful advanced ratchet system as used on festoon blinds allow the blind to be secured at any level.

Festoon and Roman blinds may be ordered in any of the prints and colourways currently offered in country furnishing cotton, chintz and drawing room fabric.

See page 171 for ordering details.

MADE TO MEASURE
BLINDS

◀ ROLLER BLINDS

In early nineteenth century England simple roller blinds of pure white cotton were used as sun-shades on large windows, sometimes with accompanying curtains.

Today, roller blinds make an attractive and easy way to screen a window, filling it neatly with a block of colour or a print, to blend in with the rest of the room.

The new Laura Ashley Made to Measure roller blind is available in a choice of prints and colourways, as illustrated, from our extensive range of country furnishing cottons.

For details on how to order see page 171.

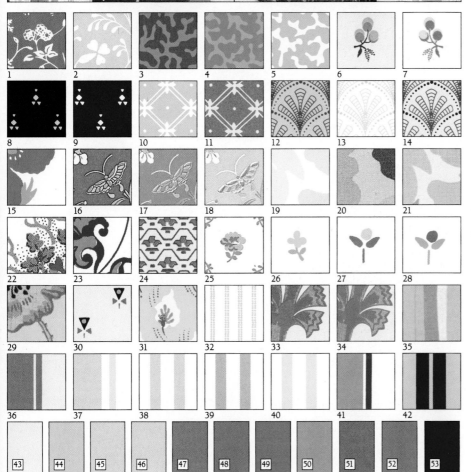

1. Wild Clematis S65 White/Moss *004017* **2.** Campion R143 White/Rose *021067* **3.** Petra F671 Crimson *357317* **4.** Petra F671 Jade *357339* **5.** Petra F671 Buttermilk *357328* **6.** Rowan F686 Sage/Dark Green/Cream *365554* **7.** Rowan F686 Light Rose/Moss/White *365533* **8.** Nutmeg S49 Sand/Navy *015019* **9.** Nutmeg S49 White/Burgundy *015084* **10.** Wickerwork L571 White/Sand *041068* **11.** Wickerwork L571 Cream/Sage *041033* **12.** Palmetto F303 Dark Green/Raspberry/Sand *184263* **13.** Palmetto F303 Aquamarine/Apricot/White *184268* **14.** Palmetto F303 Kingfisher/Burgundy/Cream *184256* **15.** Meadow Flowers F42 Poppy Multi White *078143* **16.** Floribunda L577 Multi Poppy *042094* **17.** Floribunda L577 Multi Sapphire *042195* **18.** Floribunda L577 Multi Apricot *042096* **19.** Emma C17 Multi Apricot/White *517415* **20.** Emma C17 Multi Guava/Stone *517400* **21.** Emma C17 Multi Straw/Cream *517401* **22.** Morning Parlour F474 Deep Sapphire Multi White *098497* **23.** Ming F132 China Blue/Sapphire/White *135162* **24.** Queen Anne's Needlework F10 Terracotta/Oak/Cream *070452* **25.** Kate F373 Rose/Moss/White *173080* **26.** Wood Violet P753 Mustard/Apple/White *046194* **27.** Cottage Sprig P767 Rose/Moss/White *053080* **28.** Cottage Sprig P767 Poppy/Apple/White *053169* **29.** Cordelia F537 Multi Stone *328397* **30.** Scottish Thistle F4 Burgundy/Sage/Cream *065188* **31.** Cornflowers F333 Sapphire Multi Mustard *187485* **32.** Candy Stripe G426 Rose/White *039066* **33.** Dandelion F335 Plum/Sage/Cream *302447* **34.** Dandelion F335 Terracotta/Moss/Cream *302270* **35.** Studio F792 Multi Straw/Cream *370401* **36.** Cricket Stripe F369 Terracotta/Moss/Cream *185449* **37.** Regency Stripe F374 Apricot/Aquamarine/White *197265* **38.** Brighton Rock F389 Apricot/White *174074* **39.** Brighton Rock F389 Sugar Pink/White *174127* **40.** Brighton Rock F389 Aquamarine/White *174206* **41.** Cricket Stripe F369 Sapphire/China Blue/White *185258* **42.** Regatta B10 Burgundy/Sand *086217* **43.** Cream *020110* **44.** Sand *020109* **45.** Rose *020114* **46.** Apricot *020116* **47.** Terracotta *020111* **48.** Moss *020102* **49.** Poppy *020113* **50.** Sapphire *020107* **51.** Plum *020112* **52.** Smoke *020106* **53.** Burgundy *020115*

UPHOLSTERED FURNITURE COLLECTION

Drawing inspiration from furniture of the eighteenth and nineteenth centuries, our comfortable and inviting upholstered furniture is constructed with eight-way hand-tied tempered steel coil springs, with double dowelled frames of selected kiln-dried five-quarter oak and hardwoods. Cushions consist of high-resiliency polyurethane foam that will retain its shape over many years of use, enclosed in a ticking for added protection. Back pillows are filled with soft and resilient Dacron fibre and encased in a sewn channelled ticking.

The beautifully tailored dress maker details that abound throughout our Upholstered Furniture Collection set each piece apart from the ordinary.

Our furniture is constructed to these exacting standards by Bridgeford, the renowned upholstered furniture division of Henredon.

Shown here is but a sampling of our entire furniture range. Each of these, and our other pieces, is available custom upholstered in your choice of any of our prints and solids.

▲ Sheffield Sofa in Hamilton F505 Terracotta Multi Cream *092233*
▼ Sheffield Loveseat in Simla F516 Multi Terracotta *331398*

SHEFFIELD SOFA

Product Code *7070*
Width: 86ins Depth: 41ins
Height: 38ins Arm height: 30ins

Country Furnishing Cotton	$1920
Chintz	$2195
Drawing Room Fabric/Dobby	$2485
Upholstery Fabric/Linen Union	$2625

SHEFFIELD LOVESEAT

Product Code *7071*
Width: 63ins Depth: 41ins
Height: 38ins Arm height: 30ins

Country Furnishing Cotton	$1750
Chintz	$1995
Drawing Room Fabric/Dobby	$2285
Upholstery Fabric/Linen Union	$2410

This tight-back, rolled arm silhouette features a tailored double kick-pleat skirt.

▲ Bristol Chair in **Palmetto** F303 Aquamarine/Apricot/White *184268*
▼ Dorset Ottoman in **Paisley** F477 Plum/Saddle/Cream *332264*
Devon Chair in **Emma** C17 Multi Straw/Cream *517401* ▼

BRISTOL CHAIR

Product Code 7052
Width: 36ins Depth: 36ins
Height: 32ins Arm height: 23ins

Country Furnishing Cotton	$815
Chintz	$1045
Drawing Room Fabric/Dobby	$1275
Upholstery Fabric/Linen Union	$1345

BRISTOL OTTOMAN

(Not shown) Product Code 7053
Width: 28ins Depth: 20ins
Height: 18ins

While thoroughly twentieth century in its comfort, our Bristol chair nonetheless features the hand diamond-tufted back and rolled arms of the nineteenth century upholstery. With its tailored double kick-pleat skirt, this is a lounge chair for all occasions.

DORSET OTTOMAN

Product Code 7078
Width: 30ins Depth: 30ins
Height: 18ins

Country Furnishing Cotton	$455
Chintz	$550
Drawing Room Fabric/Dobby	$640
Upholstery Fabric/Linen Union	$680

Lend an element of unexpected character to your room with our hand-tufted and flounced Dorset Ottoman adapted from a popular mid-nineteenth century French design called a 'pouf'.

DEVON CHAIR

Product Code 7082
Width: 33ins Depth: 33ins
Height: 36ins Arm height: 25ins

Country Furnishing Cotton	$815
Chintz	$1045
Drawing Room Fabric/Dobby	$1280
Upholstery Fabric/Linen Union	$1350

Victorian upholstered furniture depended on buttoning and elaborate skirt treatments to carry the design theme. In the Devon Chair — a remake of the ever-popular slipper chair — the button-back, flowing skirt, and fan-shirred arms lend the charm of a bygone era to your home.

Upholstered Furniture is made in the U.S.A.

CARLISLE SOFA

(Not shown) Product Code *7020*
Width: 87ins Depth: 37ins
Height: 33ins Arm height: 24ins

CARLISLE LOVESEAT

Product Code *7021*
Width: 65ins Depth: 37ins
Height: 33ins Arm height: 24ins
Country Furnishing Cotton $1840
Chintz $2145
Drawing Room Fabric/Dobby $2450
Upholstery Fabric/Linen Union $2575

CARLISLE CHAIR

Product Code *7022*
Width: 31ins Depth: 34ins
Height: 34ins Arm height: 25ins
Country Furnishing Cotton $910
Chintz $1140
Drawing Room Fabric/Dobby $1370
Upholstery Fabric/Linen Union $1440

CARLISLE OTTOMAN

Product Code *7023*
Width: 28ins Depth: 22ins Height: 19ins
Country Furnishing Cotton $515
Chintz $625
Drawing Room Fabric/Dobby $735
Upholstery Fabric/Linen Union $775

Here the upholsterer's art reaches its
full realisation. A pleated skirt runs fully
around each piece. The interior backs
are diamond-tufted by hand.
Available as a full sofa (not shown),
loveseat, chair and ottoman.

DUDLEY LOVESEAT

Surrey finish. Product Code *7076*
Width: 64ins Depth: 33ins
Height: 38ins Arm height: 25ins
Country Furnishing Cotton $1430
Chintz $1720
Drawing Room Fabric/Dobby $1995
Linen Union $2110

Our Dudley Loveseat in the Queen
Victoria rococo style has diamond
tufted back and front rail, and
beautifully turned legs (available in
either bleached oak or dark walnut
finishes) it is a faithful adaptation
from that gentle era.

▲ Carlisle Chair & Ottoman in **Kate** F373 Rose/Moss/White *173080*

▲ Carlisle Loveseat in **Wickerwork** L571 White/Rose *041067*
▼ Dudley Loveseat in **Malcolm** F403 Multi Cream *088395*

▲ Cambria Sofa in **Favorita** F206 Navy Multi Sand *114480*
▼ Cambria Chair in **Mr. Jones** F381 Navy/Burgundy/Sand *190261*
Kent Chair in **Cricket Stripe** F369 Sand/Navy/Cream *185262* ▼

CAMBRIA SOFA

Product Code *7030*
Width: 86ins Depth: 35ins
Height: 31ins Arm height: 26ins

Country Furnishing Cotton	$1430
Chintz	$1745
Drawing Room Fabric/Dobby	$2060
Upholstery Fabric/Linen Union	$2230

CAMBRIA LOVESEAT

(Not shown) Product Code *7031*
Width: 65ins Depth: 35ins
Height: 31ins Arm height: 26ins

CAMBRIA CHAIR

Product Code *7032*
Width: 41ins Depth: 34ins
Height: 30ins Arm height: 26ins

Country Furnishing Cotton	$910
Chintz	$1140
Drawing Room Fabric/Dobby	$1370
Upholstery Fabric/Linen Union	$1440

The gentle crest of these camelback designs harken back to their eighteenth century ancestors. Our Cambria grouping was copied from similar upholstery found in Mrs. Ashley's home and features an 8 inch flounced skirt and generous roll arms.

KENT CHAIR

Product Code *7017*
Width: 31ins Depth: 33ins
Height: 32ins Arm height: 25ins

Country Furnishing Cotton	$815
Chintz	$1045
Drawing Room Fabric/Dobby	$1280
Upholstery Fabric/Linen Union	$1350

With its camelback design and rolled arms our Kent Chair follows the silhouette of an eighteenth century club chair. We have added the corner flounced skirt and deeper seating for twentieth century comfort.

Upholstered Furniture is made in the U.S.A.

LAURA ASHLEY
INTERIOR DESIGN SERVICE

Plan your Laura Ashley interiors with the assistance of our Interior Design Service. In the New York, Boston and San Francisco areas we offer a complete Interior Design Service that can assist you on one room or your entire home. Our Interior Designers will consult with you on your needs and specify not only our home furnishings, but anything and everything needed to complete your Laura Ashley interiors.

New York: 714 Madison Avenue, New York, N.Y. 10021 (212) 735-5010

Boston: 83 Newbury Street, Boston, Massachusetts 02116 (617) 424-6808

San Francisco: 563 Sutter Street, San Francisco, California 94102 (415) 788-0796

LAURA ASHLEY
INTERIOR DESIGN CONSULTANT

In the Chicago area our in-shop Interior Design Consultant will advise you on your Laura Ashley design alternatives when you visit one of our Illinois shops and will be able to help you co-ordinate the perfect Laura Ashley interior for your home.

Chicago: (312) 951-8004

During 1986 we plan the addition of more Interior Design Consultants in other Laura Ashley shops throughout the country. Please call this Toll Free number for the Laura Ashley Interior Design Consultant nearest you:

Toll free: 1 (800) 367-2000

Sapphire blue is the colour theme for this bathroom, from the glossy cushion, and the tiles, to the tapestry cushion and the tissue box holder.

Pick out one colour in a pattern, in this case the pink from the matching fabric and wallpaper. Use it for small details like the ribbon surrounding the lining to the doll's pram or for larger details like the softly patterned pink country furnishing cotton that lines the drape over the child's cot.

Feel confident about mixing pattern with pattern. The colours make the main link in this simple black and white Welsh scullery where the gentle trellised wallpaper is sharpened with the crisp black and white striped fabric.

From modest country scullery to the smartest of bachelor apartments, the first part of this catalogue demonstrates vividly how fabrics, wallcoverings and paints can be used in a variety of ways to create different effects.

Most importantly it shows how colours mix and match exactly across the various products, giving a huge range of co-ordination possibilities. This means several different fabrics can be used in a room, plus wallcoverings and paint. Then there are tiles and borders, trimmings, and accessories

like cushions and lamps. Everything harmonises from a colour point of view. So you can work through the elements of a room knowing everything can be put together as professionally as an interior decorator to give an individual look.

Knowing that everything works together gives you a greater freedom of choice and confidence when it comes to planning rooms. Playing with pattern and colour, room schemes of all kinds can be put together to give a distinctive look.

Each year we introduce new fabrics to our ranges, many of which are based on historical designs. Laura Ashley feels strongly that the patterns of the past still have an important place today. This year the design spectrum has been broadened to introduce a crop of fabrics with larger and bolder designs, like the Paisley with its masculine feel. The new Chinoiserie fabric introduces the atmosphere of an eighteenth century English drawing room. Both of these patterns enhance the range of classical designs and

Carry a pattern through a room — here the blind matches the wallpaper, then is repeated again on the tiles, on the walls and on the floor.

Pick out not just one, but several of the colours from a multi-coloured fabric. Here the crimson, buttermilk and jade colours of the bedspread are picked out and used elsewhere in the room: buttermilk in the new Chinese fretwork pattern for the sofa, and all three colours for the plump cushions.

Remember the smallest details. Merely changing the colour of piping on a cushion can make all the difference. Here the blue of the richly coloured main fabric is used to pipe cushions on the bed.

are steeped in the history of design. Through the centuries designers have always drawn on the ideas of yesterday, adapting them in many ways. These new additions work in with the more familiar sprig and dimity designs inspired by early Victorian dress fabrics and which have made Laura Ashley famous the world over.

While the first part of the catalogue is designed to provide you with ideas, the next two sections are there to help put these ideas into action. In the second section the many fabrics and products are grouped according to type, so you can see what the whole range has to offer. In the final part, everything is grouped together in colour terms — a great help for co-ordinating decoration ideas.

To begin, take inspiration from our rooms in the early part of the catalogue. Then browse through the products section. Perhaps you want to decorate a bedroom. Select those products you need to create the right effect. Look for wallcovering, curtain fabric, a patchwork quilt, bedlinen, lampshades and other accessories. Now turn to the prints and colourways section to find the full range of co-ordinating possibilities. You will find that in a multi-coloured design you can pick out any one of the colours and emphasise it with the accessory fabrics, borders, tiles and paint to match.

To demonstrate the many possibilities, we have selected details of some of the rooms from the first section of the catalogue. See how these work and then try it out for yourself.

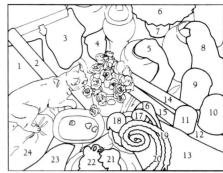

1. Square Piped Chintz Cushion **Jade**
2. Wallpaper **Pagoda** Crimson Multi White
3. Chintz **Crystal** Crimson Multi White
4. Country Furnishing Cotton **Fretwork** Multi Smoke
5. Country Furnishing Cotton **Fretwork** Multi Crimson
6. Firm Pleated Lampshade **Petra** Jade
7. Large Crackle Glaze Lampbase **Cream**
8. Country Furnishing Cotton **Oriana** Multi Crimson
9. Flat Paint **Pale Jade**
10. Flat Paint **Pale Buttermilk**
11. Gloss Paint **Crimson**
12. Country Furnishing Cotton **Petra** Buttermilk
13. Chintz **Chinoiserie** Kingfisher Multi Stone
14. Wallpaper **Cirque** Buttermilk
15. Wallpaper **Petra** Jade
16. Folded Bias Binding **Jade**
17. Folded Bias Binding **Crimson**
18. Folded Bias Binding **Buttermilk**
19. Cord Tie-Back **Cream**
20. Cord Tie-Back **Crimson**
21. Fringing **Crimson**
22. Plain Gimp **Crimson**
23. Country Furnishing Cotton **Petra** Crimson
24. Country Furnishing Cotton **Attic** Mulberry/Sand/White

CRIMSON BUTTERMILK & JADE

CRIMSON

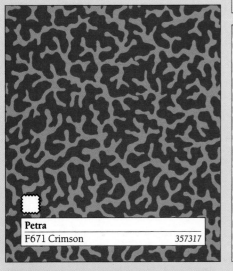

Petra
F671 Crimson   357317

Petra
F671 Buttermilk   357328

Crimson
020317

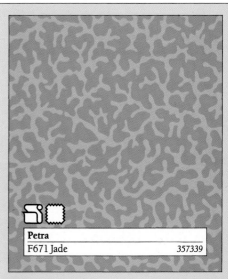

Petra
F671 Jade   357339

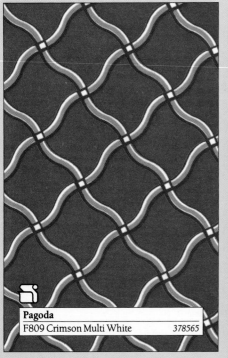

Pagoda
F809 Crimson Multi White   378565

Cirque
F782 Buttermilk   371328

Crystal
F784 Crimson Multi White   381565

 WALLPAPER   VINYL WALL-COVERING   COUNTRY FURNISHING COTTON    DRAWING ROOM FABRIC   LINEN UNION   DOBBY   UPHOLSTERY FABRIC   CHINTZ

BUTTERMILK

Fretwork
F772 Multi Buttermilk   376409

Buttermilk
020328

Pale Buttermilk 020331

Fretwork
F772 Multi Smoke   376417

Fretwork
F772 Multi Crimson   376410

Chinoiserie
F812 Kingfisher Multi Stone   382479

JADE

Jade
020339

Pale Jade 020332

Oriana
F771 Multi Crimson   366410

Cirque
F782 Grey/White   371076

 PLASTIC COATED FABRIC   GLOSS PAINT   FLAT PAINT   CERAMIC TILES   LAMP-SHADES   DINING COLLECTION   CUSHIONS   BEDLINEN

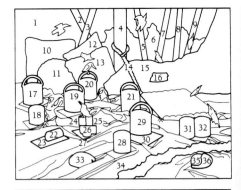

1. Country Furn. Cotton **Shepherd's Purse** Smoke/Cream
2. Linen Union **Florentina** Smoke Multi Cream
3. Drawing Room Fabric **Albert** Oak Multi Sand
4. Country Furnishing Cotton **Emma** Multi Guava/Stone
5. Country Furnishing Cotton **Edward** Kingfisher/Stone
6. Country Furnishing Cotton **Cordelia** Multi Stone
7. Country Furnishing Cotton **Studio** Multi Guava/Stone
8. Country Furnishing Cotton **Sea Spray** Kingfisher/Stone
9. Country Furnishing Cotton **Harbour** Kingfisher/Stone
10. Flat Bordered Cushion Smoke with **Stratford** Border
11. Round Frilled Cushion **Paisley** Smoke/Kingfisher/Cream
12. Square Piped Chintz Cushion Smoke
13. Sq. Frilled Cushion **Palmetto** Kingfisher/Burgundy/Cr.
14. Cord Tie-Back Smoke
15. Lattice Patchwork Quilt Smoke
16. Fringing Smoke
17. Flat Paint Stone
18. Gloss Paint Kingfisher
19. Flat Paint Light Smoke
20. Flat Paint Light Guava
21. Flat Paint Light Kingfisher
22. Wallpaper Border **Harbour** Kingfisher/Stone
23. Border Tile Cream
24. Wallpaper Border **Stratford** Smoke Multi Stone
25. Wallpaper Border **Byron** Cloud Blue/Oak
26. Wallpaper Borders **Minuet** Smoke/Cream
27. Wall Tile Cream
28. Gloss Paint Smoke
29. Flat Paint Cream
30. Floor & Wall Tile Cream
31. Gloss Paint Cream
32. Gloss Paint Stone
33. Bias Binding Guava
34. Chintz Smoke
35. Bias Binding Cream
36. Bias Binding Smoke

KINGFISHER & SMOKE

KINGFISHER

Sara Jane
F798 Kingfisher Multi Stone　　368479

Damask
F526 Kingfisher/Smoke　　326281

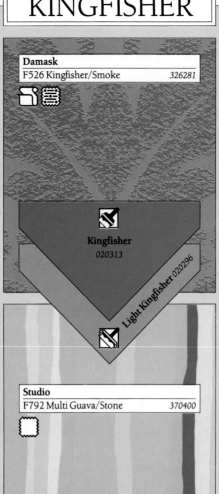

Palmetto
F303 Kingfisher/Burgundy/Cream　184256

Kingfisher
020313

Light Kingfisher 020296

Emma
C17 Multi Guava/Stone　　517400

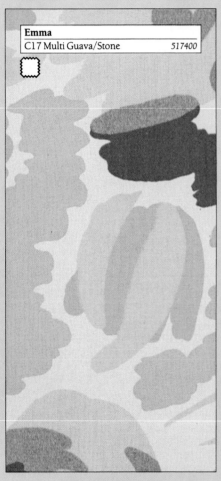

Sophie
F614 Multi Guava/Stone　　352400

Studio
F792 Multi Guava/Stone　　370400

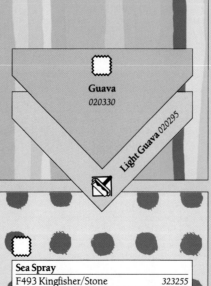

Guava
020330

Light Guava 020295

Harbour
F490 Kingfisher/Stone　　324255

Sea Spray
F493 Kingfisher/Stone　　323255

Edward
F456 Kingfisher/Stone　　325255

 WALLPAPER　　 VINYL WALL-COVERING　　 COUNTRY FURNISHING COTTON　　 DRAWING ROOM FABRIC　　 LINEN UNION　　 DOBBY　　 UPHOLSTERY FABRIC　　 CHINTZ

SMOKE

Petite Fleur
R150 Cream/Smoke   *026014*

Petite Fleur
R150 Smoke/Cream   *026013*

Albert
F288 Oak Multi Sand   *339502*

Paisley
F477 Smoke/Kingfisher/Cream   *332500*

Shepherd's Purse
R193 Smoke/Cream   *028013*

Smoke
020106

Light Smoke 020345

Cordelia
F537 Multi Stone   *328397*

Natural
020325

Stone
020300

Cream
020110

Infinity
F111 Smoke/Cream   *137013*

Wild Clematis
S65 Cream/Smoke   *004014*

Wild Clematis
S65 Smoke/Cream   *004013*

Grapes
F62 Smoke Multi Cream   *158247*

Florentina
F358 Smoke Multi Cream   *192247*

 PLASTIC COATED FABRIC
 GLOSS PAINT
 FLAT PAINT
 CERAMIC TILES
 LAMP-SHADES
 DINING COLLECTION
 CUSHIONS
 BEDLINEN

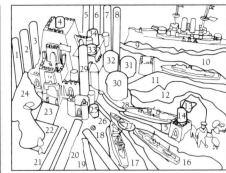

1	Vinyl Wallcovering **Trellis** Sand/White
2	Vinyl Wallcovering **Wickerwork** Sand/White
3	Vinyl Wallcovering **Wickerwork** White/Sand
4	Wallpaper Border **Swinburne** Burgundy/Navy/Sand
5	Wallpaper **Marble** Greengage Multi Stone
6	Vinyl Wallcovering **Nutmeg** Navy/Sand
7	Vinyl Wallcovering **Nutmeg** Sand/Navy
8	Wallpaper **Nutmeg** White/Sand
9	Fabric Border **Trompe** Navy/Sand
10	Country Furnishing Cotton **Nutmeg** Sand/Navy
11	Country Furnishing Cotton **Simla** Multi Allspice
12	Country Furnishing Cotton **Indienne** Multi Allspice
13	Fabric Border **Polka** Sand/Cream/White
14	Wallpaper Border **Byron** Sand/Navy
15	Country Furnishing Cotton **Navy**
16	Country Furn. Cotton **Cricket Stripe** Sand/Navy/Cream
17	Country Furn. Cotton **Stitchwort** Navy/Burgundy/Sand
18	Wallpaper **Salon** Sand/White
19	Wallpaper **Shepherd's Purse** Sand/White
20	Vinyl Wallcovering **Rectory Garden** Rasp./Moss/Stone
21	Vinyl Wallcovering **Bembridge** Burgundy/Navy/Sand
22	Floor & Wall Tile **Bembridge** Burgundy/Navy/Sand
23	Wall Tile **Bembridge** Burgundy/Navy/Sand
24	Towel **Burgundy** edged with **Regatta** Burgundy/Sand
25	Wallpaper Border **Byron** White/Sand
26	Folded Bias Binding **Navy**
27	Braid **Sand/Cream**
28	Braid **Navy/Burgundy**
29	Vinyl Wallcovering **Mr. Jones** Navy/Burgundy/Sand
30	Flat Paint **Sand**
31	Gloss Paint **Navy**
32	Gloss Paint **Sand**
33	Wallpaper Border **Polka** Sand/Cream/White
34	Wallpaper Border **Clifford** Dark Silver Multi White

SAND, NAVY & BURGUNDY

SAND

Wickerwork
L571 White/Sand   *041068*

Wickerwork
L571 Sand/White   *041038*

Shepherd's Purse
R193 Sand/White   *028038*

Nutmeg
S49 White/Sand   *015068*

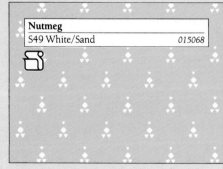

Joy
F125 Sand Multi White   *141139*

Sand
020109

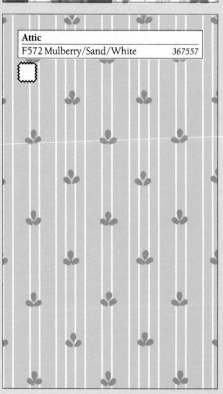

Attic
F572 Mulberry/Sand/White   *367557*

Trellis
P768 Sand/Cream   *054210*

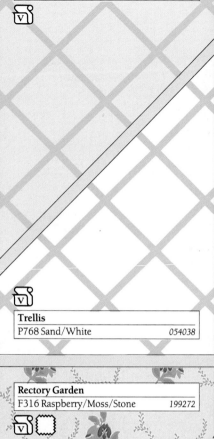

Trellis
P768 Sand/White   *054038*

Rectory Garden
F316 Raspberry/Moss/Stone   *199272*

Salon
F112 Sand/White   *129038*

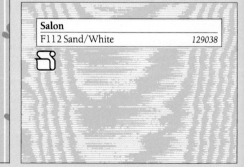

 WALLPAPER   VINYL WALL-COVERING   COUNTRY FURNISHING COTTON    DRAWING ROOM FABRIC   LINEN UNION   DOBBY   UPHOLSTERY FABRIC   CHINTZ

NAVY

Emmeline
F127 Sand Multi White   *147139*

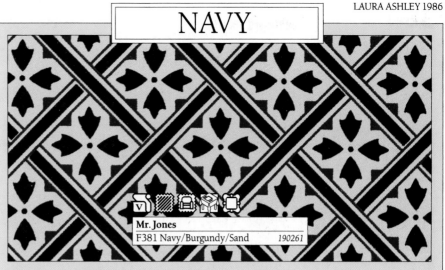

Mr. Jones
F381 Navy/Burgundy/Sand   *190261*

Scottish Thistle
F4 Navy/Sage/Sand   *065562*

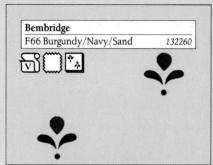

Bembridge
F66 Burgundy/Navy/Sand   *132260*

English Garden
F367 Taupe Multi White   *178486*

Emperor
F210 Navy Multi Stone   *145231*

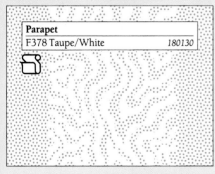

Parapet
F378 Taupe/White   *180130*

Stitchwort
F320 Navy/Burgundy/Sand   *191261*

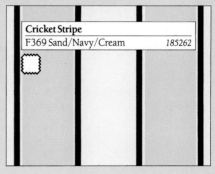

Cricket Stripe
F369 Sand/Navy/Cream   *185262*

 PLASTIC COATED FABRIC   GLOSS PAINT   FLAT PAINT   CERAMIC TILES   LAMP-SHADES   DINING COLLECTION   CUSHIONS   BEDLINEN

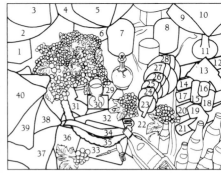

1	Large Octag. Crackle Glaze Base (Not available in U.S.A.)
2	Large Soft Pleated Lampshade (Not available in U.S.A.)
3	Country Furnishing Cotton **Grand Paisley** Multi Tan
4	Large Soft Pleated Lampshade (Not available in U.S.A.)
5	Country Furnishing Cotton **Oak Leaves** Multi Burgundy
6	Large Octag. Crackle Glaze Base (Not available in U.S.A.)
7	Flat Paint **Burgundy**
8	Flat Paint **Light Sage**
9	Column Lampbase & Shade **Burgundy**
10	Country Furnishing Cotton **Oak Leaves** Multi Dark Green
11	Wooden Column Lampbase **Burgundy/Sand**
12	Vinyl Wallcovering **Palmetto** Dk. Green/Rasp./Sand
13	Wallpaper Border **Trompe** Tan/Cream
14	Wallpaper **Albert** Dark Green Multi Sage
15	Wallpaper Border **Byron** Sand/Burgundy
16	Wallpaper Border **Polka** Burgundy/Saddle/Cream
17	Vinyl Wallcovering **Scottish Thistle** Burg./Sage/Cream
18	Wallpaper Border **Byron** Sand/Dark Green
19	Wallpaper Border **Stratford** Tan Multi Sand
20	Wallpaper **Basketweave** Burgundy/Cream
21	Wallpaper **Nutmeg** White/Burgundy
22	Drawing Room Fabric **Favorita** Dark Green Multi Sand
23	Braid **Dark Green/Burgundy/Sand**
24	Plain Gimp **Burgundy**
25	Braid **Sage**
26	Folded Bias Binding **Burgundy**
27	Folded Bias Binding **Sage**
28	Folded Bias Binding **Dark Green**
29	Fabric Border **Polka** Burgundy/Saddle/Cream
30	Coaster **Mr. Jones** Navy/Burgundy/Sand
31	Fabric Border **Trompe** Burgundy/Sand
32	Large Place-Mat **Mr. Jones** Navy/Burgundy/Sand
33	Small Place-Mat **Mr. Jones** Navy/Burgundy/Sand
34	Fringing **Burgundy**
35	Cord Tie-Back **Burgundy**
36	Drawing Room Fabric **Regency Stripe** Dark Green/Burgundy/Sand
37	Flat Bordered Cushion **Burgundy** with **Stratford** Border
38	Square Piped Cushion **Paisley** Burgundy/Navy/Tan
39	Square Piped Cushion **Grand Paisley** Multi Navy
40	Square Piped Cushion **Grand Paisley** Multi Burgundy

SAND, NAVY BURGUNDY & DARK GREEN

BURGUNDY

Shamrock
F711 Burgundy/Dark Green/Tan   *375556*

Tan
020122

Oak Leaves
F785 Multi Burgundy   *364243*

Grand Paisley
F706 Multi Tan   *363411*

Grand Paisley
F706 Multi Burgundy   *363243*

Paisley
F477 Burgundy/Navy/Tan   *332555*

Regatta
B10 Burgundy/Sand   *086217*

 WALLPAPER   VINYL WALL-COVERING   COUNTRY FURNISHING COTTON   DRAWING ROOM FABRIC   LINEN UNION   DOBBY   UPHOLSTERY FABRIC   CHINTZ

NAVY

Favorita
F206 Dark Green Multi Navy   *144564*

Favorita
F206 Navy Multi Sand   *144480*

Navy
020104

Grand Paisley
F706 Multi Navy   *363413*

Nutmeg
S49 Navy/Sand   *015020*

Nutmeg
S49 Sand/Navy   *015019*

 PLASTIC COATED FABRIC   GLOSS PAINT   FLAT PAINT   CERAMIC TILES   LAMP-SHADES   DINING COLLECTION   CUSHIONS   BEDLINEN

BURGUNDY

Basketweave
F500 Burgundy/Cream   *341208*

Venetia
F99 Burgundy/Gold   *146232*

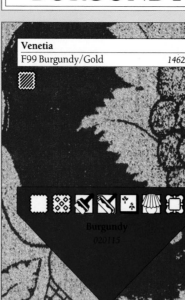

Burgundy
020115

Florentina
F358 Burgundy Multi Stone   *192481*

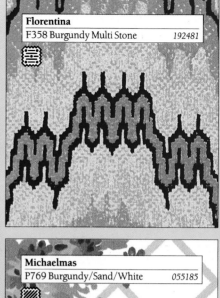

Indienne
F538 Multi Allspice   *333399*

Michaelmas
P769 Burgundy/Sand/White   *055185*

Simla
F516 Multi Allspice   *331399*

Trellis
P768 Sand/White   *054038*

Nutmeg
S49 White/Burgundy   *015084*

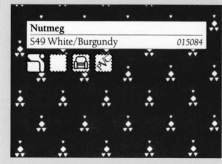

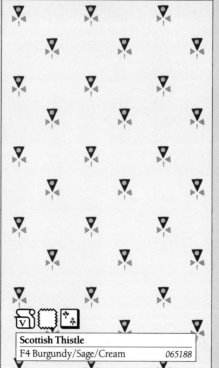

Scottish Thistle
F4 Burgundy/Sage/Cream   *065188*

Nutmeg
S49 Burgundy/White   *015086*

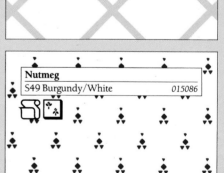

DARK GREEN

Florentina
F358 Dark Green Multi Stone   *192496*

Favorita
F206 Dark Green Multi Sand   *144230*

Palmetto
F303 Dark Green/Raspberry/Sand   *184263*

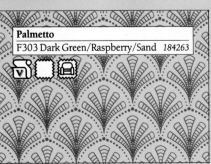

Damask
F526 Dark Green/Mid Green   *326499*

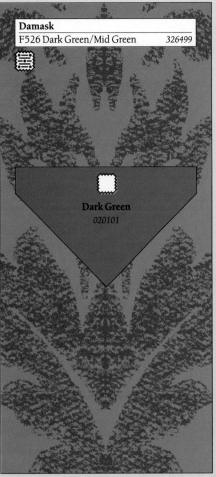

Dark Green
020101

Albert
F288 Dark Green Multi Sage   *339563*

Marble
F628 Greengage Multi Stone   *299505*

Oak Leaves
F785 Multi Dark Green   *364414*

Regency Stripe
F374 Dark Green/Burgundy/Sand   *197446*

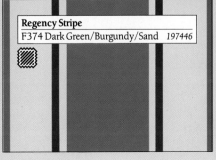

 PLASTIC COATED FABRIC

 GLOSS PAINT

 FLAT PAINT

 CERAMIC TILES

 LAMP-SHADES

 DINING COLLECTION

 CUSHIONS

 BEDLINEN

1	Firm Pleated Lampshade (Not available in U.S.A.)
2	Square Piped Chintz Cushion **Plum**
3	Flat Paint **Cream**
4	Gloss Paint **Plum & Cream**
5	Drawing Room Fabric **Malcolm** Multi Cream
6	Drawing Room Fabric **Michaelmas** Plum/Sand/Cream
7	Sq. Piped Chintz Cushion **Wh. Bower** Dk.Green Multi Cr.

8	Appliqué Cushion **Plum** with **Minuet** Border
9	Country Furn. Cotton **Dandelion** Plum/Sage/Cream
10	Country Furnishing Cotton **Wickerwork** Cream/Sage
11	Country Furnishing Cotton **Nutmeg** Cream/Plum
12	Country Furnishing Cotton **Nutmeg** Cream/Sage
13	Lattice Patchwork Quilt **Plum**
14	Wallpaper Border **Trompe** Sage/Cream

SAGE & PLUM

15 Wallpaper Borders **Minuet** Plum/Cream	22 Vinyl Wallcovering **Palmetto** Sage/Cherry/White
16 Wallpaper Border **Bulrush** Plum Multi Cream	23 Wallpaper **Rowan** Sage/Dark Green/Cream
17 Country Furn. Cotton **Rowan** Sage/Dark Green/Cream	24 Vinyl Wallcovering **Wild Clematis** Plum/Cream
18 Fabric Border **Bulrush** Plum Multi Cream	25 Vinyl Wallcovering **Trellis** Sand/Cream
19 Vinyl Wallcovering **Dandelion** Plum/Sage/Cream	26 Vinyl Wallcovering **Nutmeg** Plum/Cream
20 Wallpaper **Wickerwork** Sage/Cream	27 Cord Tie-Back **Plum**
21 Wallpaper **Nutmeg** Sage/Cream	28 Round Frilled Cushion **Paisley** Plum/Saddle/Cream

SAGE

Nutmeg
S49 Sage/Cream   015032

Palmetto
F303 Sage/Cherry/White   184273

Sage
020123

Light Sage 020350

Nutmeg
S49 Cream/Sage   015033

Rowan
F686 Sage/Dark Green/Cream   365554

Wickerwork
L571 Sage/Cream   041032

Wickerwork
L571 Cream/Sage   041033

White Bower
F364 Dark Green Multi Cream   195482

 WALLPAPER
 VINYL WALL-COVERING
 COUNTRY FURNISHING COTTON
 DRAWING ROOM FABRIC
 LINEN UNION
 DOBBY
 UPHOLSTERY FABRIC
 CHINTZ

PLUM

Michaelmas
P769 Plum/Sand/Cream   055223

Dandelion
F335 Plum/Sage/Cream   302447

Plum
020112

Light Plum *020347*

Paisley
F477 Plum/Saddle/Cream   332264

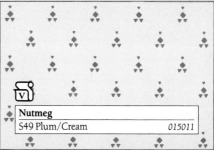

Nutmeg
S49 Plum/Cream   015011

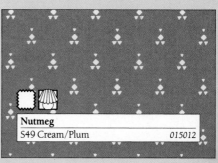

Nutmeg
S49 Cream/Plum   015012

Trellis
P768 Sand/Cream   054210

Malcolm
F403 Multi Cream   088395

Wild Clematis
S65 Plum/Cream   004011

Wild Clematis
S65 Cream/Plum   004012

 PLASTIC COATED FABRIC   GLOSS PAINT   FLAT PAINT   CERAMIC TILES   LAMP-SHADES    DINING COLLECTION   CUSHIONS   BEDLINEN

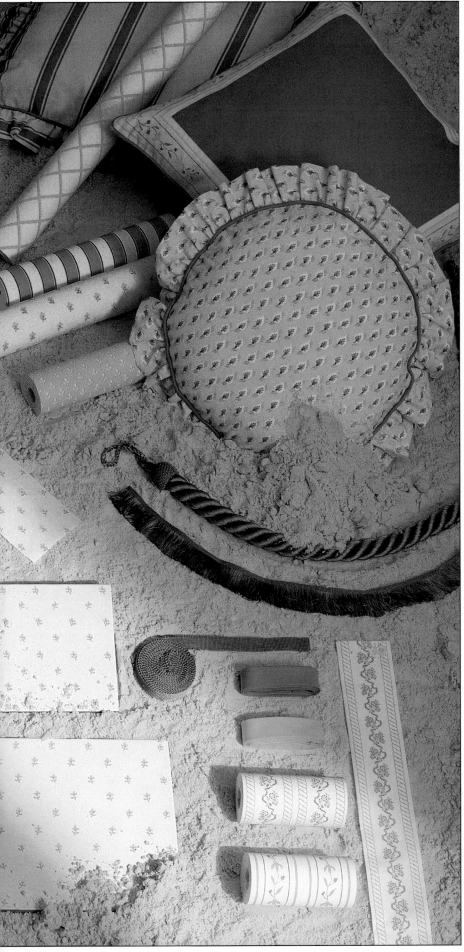

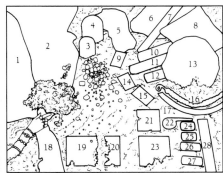

1	Chintz **Carousel** Mustard Multi Sapphire
2	Lattice Patchwork Quilt **Sapphire**
3	Gloss Paint **Sapphire**
4	Flat Paint **Soft Sapphire**
5	Country Furn. Cotton **Wind Spray** Sapphire Multi White
6	Square Frilled Cushion **Riviera** Sapphire/Mustard
7	Wallpaper **Trellis** Mustard/White
8	Appliqué Cushion **Sapphire** with **Polka** Border
9	Country Furnishing Cotton **Trefoil** White/Mustard
10	Vinyl Wallcovering **Cricket Stripe** Sapph./Ch. Blue/Wh.
11	Vinyl Wallcovering **Wood Violet** Mustard/Apple/White
12	Wallpaper **Trefoil** White/Mustard
13	Rd. Frilled Cushion **Cornflowers** Sapphire Multi Mustard
14	Country Furn. Cotton **Wood Violet** Sapphire/Apple/Wh.
15	Country Furn. Cotton **Wood Violet** Mustard/Apple/Wh.
16	Cord Tie-Back **Sapphire**
17	Fringing **Sapphire**
18	Country Furnishing Cotton **Emma** Multi Sapphire White
19	Floor & Wall Tile **Sapphire**
20	Border Tile **Sapphire**
21	Wall Tile **Wood Violet** Mustard/Apple/White
22	Plain Gimp **Sapphire**
23	Floor & Wall Tile **Wood Violet** Mustard/Apple/White
24	Bias Binding **Sapphire**
25	Bias Binding **Mustard**
26	Wallpaper Borders **Minuet** Sapphire/White
27	Wallpaper Borders **Polka** Mustard Multi White
28	Fabric Border **Minuet** Sapphire/White

SAPPHIRE & MUSTARD

SAPPHIRE

Kate
F373 Sapphire/Apple/White   *173190*

Ming
F132 China Blue/Sapphire/White   *135162*

Bembridge
F66 Sapphire/Mid Blue/White   *132222*

Sapphire
020107

Soft Sapphire 020291

Wickerwork
L571 Sapphire/White   *041072*

Polly
F511 Cherry Multi White   *322244*

Morning Parlour
F474 Deep Sapphire Multi White   *098497*

Wickerwork
L571 White/Sapphire   *041073*

 WALLPAPER
 VINYL WALL-COVERING
 COUNTRY FURNISHING COTTON
 DRAWING ROOM FABRIC
 LINEN UNION
 DOBBY
 UPHOLSTERY FABRIC
 CHINTZ

SAPPHIRE

Candy Stripe
G426 Sapphire/White   039072

Cricket Stripe
F369 Sapphire/China Blue/White   185258

Regatta
B10 Sapphire/White   086072

Wood Violet
P753 Sapphire/Apple/White   046190

Campion
R143 Sapphire/White   021072

Floribunda
L577 Multi Sapphire   042195

Campion
R143 White/Sapphire   021073

SAPPHIRE

Cornflowers
F333 Sapphire Multi Mustard   *187485*

Emma
C17 Multi Sapphire/White   *517416*

Riviera
F222 Sapphire/Mustard   *131221*

Wind Spray
P784 Sapphire Multi White   *057137*

Apple
020103

 WALLPAPER   VINYL WALL-COVERING   COUNTRY FURNISHING COTTON   DRAWING ROOM FABRIC   LINEN UNION   DOBBY   UPHOLSTERY FABRIC   CHINTZ

MUSTARD

Carousel
F813 Mustard Multi Sapphire   *383567*

Mustard
020118

Trefoil
P752 White/Mustard   *045001*

Trellis
P768 Mustard/White   *054005*

Wood Violet
P753 Mustard/Apple/White   *046194*

 PLASTIC COATED FABRIC

 GLOSS PAINT

 FLAT PAINT

 CERAMIC TILES

 LAMP-SHADES

 DINING COLLECTION

 CUSHIONS

 BEDLINEN

1 Country Furn. Cotton **Meadow Flowers** Poppy Multi White	12 Country Furnishing Cotton **Cherries** Black/White
2 Country Furnishing Cotton **Floribunda** Multi Poppy	13 Wall/Floor & Wall Tiles **White**
3 Country Furnishing Cotton **Poppy**	14 Wall Tiles **Domino** Black/White
4 Country Furnishing Cotton **Marquee** Black/White	15 Floor & Wall Tiles **Pavilion** Black/White
5 Country Furn. Cotton **Cottage Sprig** Poppy/Apple/White	16 Flat Paint **White**. Gloss Paint **Poppy & White**
6 Country Furnishing Cotton **Summertime** Multi Poppy	17 Square Piped Chintz Cushion **Poppy**
7 Wallpaper **Cherries** Black/White	18 Wall/Floor & Wall Tiles **Cottage Sprig** Poppy/Apple/White
8 Vinyl Wallcovering **Cottage Sprig** Poppy/Apple/White	19 Fabric Border **Harebell** Poppy/Apple/White
9 Wallpaper **Meadow Flowers** Poppy Multi White	20 Bias Binding **Poppy**
10 Vinyl Wallcovering & Country Furn. Cott. **Floribunda** Mult. Wh.	21 Wallpaper Border **Polka** Poppy Multi White
11 Wall/Floor & Wall Tiles **Pavilion** Poppy/Mustard/Apple/Denim	22 Wallpaper Border **Domino** Black/White

POPPY

Floribunda
L577 Multi Poppy   *042094*

Summertime
F557 Multi Poppy   *336094*

Floribunda
L577 Multi White   *042242*

Cottage Sprig
P767 Poppy/Apple/White   *053169*

Meadow Flowers
F42 Poppy Multi White   *078143*

Poppy
020113

BLACK

Marquee
F556 Black/White   *334027*

Cherries
F805 Black/White   *374027*

 WALLPAPER   VINYL WALL-COVERING   COUNTRY FURNISHING COTTON   DRAWING ROOM FABRIC   LINEN UNION   DOBBY   UPHOLSTERY FABRIC   CHINTZ

 PLASTIC COATED FABRIC   GLOSS PAINT   FLAT PAINT   CERAMIC TILES   LAMP-SHADES   DINING COLLECTION   CUSHIONS   BEDLINEN

1. Country Furnishing Cotton **Marquee** Tropical Green/White
2. Country Furnishing Cotton **Marquee** Denim/White
3. Country Furnishing Cotton **Dandelion** Denim/Tropical Green/White
4. Wallpaper **Marquee** Tropical Green/White
5. Vinyl Wallcovering **Cottage Sprig** Denim/Tropical Green/White
6. Wallpaper **Trellis** Tropical Green/White
7. Wallpaper Border **Bulrush** Denim Multi White
8. Fabric Border **Bulrush** Denim Multi White
9. Country Furnishing Cotton **Tropical Green**
10. Floor & Wall Tile **Trellis** Apple/White
11. Border Tile **White**
12. Country Furnishing Cotton **Palmetto** Denim/Tropical Green/White
13. Wall Tiles **Pavilion** Poppy/Mustard/Apple/Denim
14. Floor & Wall Tile **Pavilion** Poppy/Mustard/Apple/Denim
15. Chintz **Lily of the Valley** Tropical Green Multi Stone
16. Floor & Wall Tile **Domino** Denim/White
17. Wall Tiles **Domino** Denim/White
18. Gloss Paint **White**
19. Bias Binding **Denim**
20. Bias Binding **Tropical Green**
21. Country Furnishing Cotton **Denim**

DENIM

Marquee
F556 Tropical Green/White — 334274

Palmetto
F303 Denim/Tropical Green/White *184448*

Marquee
F556 Denim/White — 334283

Lily of the Valley
F487 Tropical Green Multi Stone — *093508*

Dandelion
F335 Denim/Tropical Green/White *302448*

Denim
020525

TROPICAL GREEN

Trellis
P768 Tropical Green/White — *054274*

Tropical Green
020299

Cottage Sprig
P767 Denim/Tropical Green/White *053448*

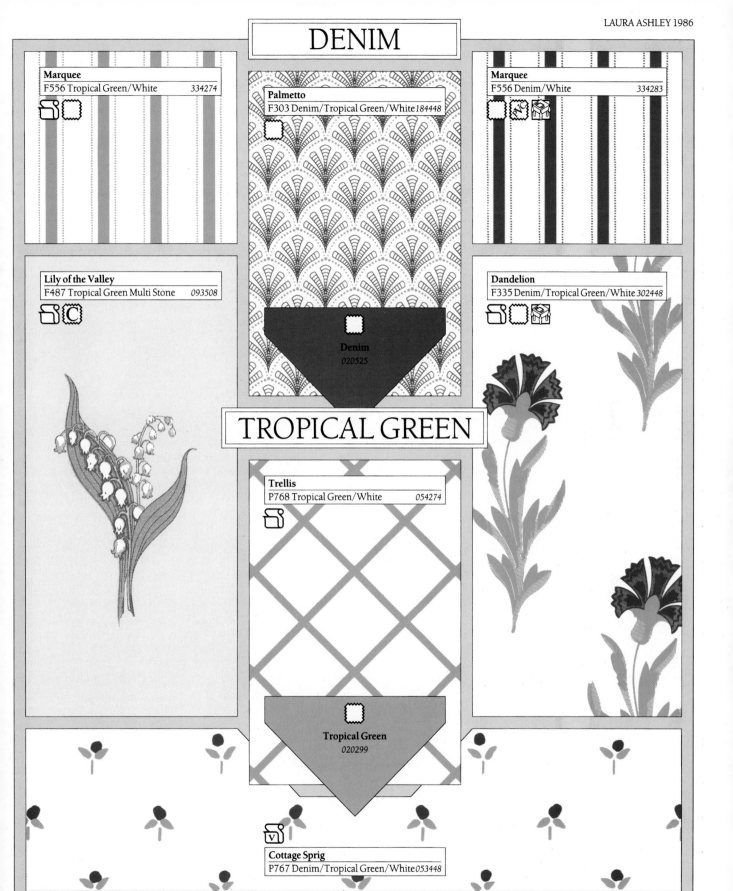

WALLPAPER	VINYL WALL-COVERING	COUNTRY FURNISHING COTTON
DRAWING ROOM FABRIC	LINEN UNION	DOBBY
UPHOLSTERY FABRIC	CHINTZ	
 PLASTIC COATED FABRIC	GLOSS PAINT	FLAT PAINT
CERAMIC TILES	LAMP-SHADES	DINING COLLECTION
CUSHIONS	BEDLINEN	

1	Country Furnishing Cotton **Simla** Multi Terracotta
2	Country Furnishing Cotton **Wild Clematis** White/Moss
3	Country Furnishing Cotton **Milfoil** Cream/Terracotta
4	Country Furnishing Cotton **Petra** Moss
5	Fabric Border **Harvest** Terracotta Multi Cream
6	Country Furn. Cotton **Maypole** Terracotta Multi Cream
7	Drawing Room Fabric **Emperor** Terracotta Multi Cream
8	Country Furnishing Cotton **Tulips** Multi Stone
9	Wallpaper **Cricket Stripe** Terracotta/Moss/Cream
10	Wallpaper **Nutmeg** Moss/White
11	Wallpaper **Wild Clematis** Moss/White
12	Wallpaper **Queen Anne's Needlework** Terracotta/Oak/Cream
13	Vinyl Wallcovering **Wood Violet** Terracotta/Moss/Cr.
14	Wallpaper **Petite Fleur** Terracotta/Cream
15	Vinyl Wallcovering **Dandelion** Terracotta/Moss/Cream
16	Vinyl Wallcovering **Tulips** Multi Stone
17	Square Frilled Cushion **Cricket Stripe** Terracotta/Moss/Cream
18	Fabric Border **Bulrush** Terracotta Multi Cream
19	Fabric Border **Key** Terracotta/Tan/Cream
20	Firm Pleated Lampshade (Not available in U.S.A.) Large Crackle Glaze Lampbase (Not available in U.S.A.)
21	Bedside Lampshade (Not available in U.S.A.) Bedside Crackle Glaze Lampase (Not available in U.S.A.)
22	Small Lampshade (Not available in U.S.A.) Small Lampbase (Not available in U.S.A.)
23	Wall Tiles **Cream**
24	Wall Tiles **Terracotta**
25	Floor & Wall Tiles **Cream**
26	Border Tiles **Cream**
27	Gloss Paint **Moss & Cream**
28	Flat Paint **Light Terracotta & Cream**
29	Round Frilled Cushion **Dandelion** Terracotta/Moss/Cream
30	Wallpaper Borders **Key** Terracotta/Tan/Cream
31	Wallpaper Borders **Polka** Tan/Terracotta/Cream
32	Wallpaper Border **Harvest** Terracotta Multi Cream
33	Wallpaper Border **Bulrush** Terracotta Multi Cream
34	Chintz **Hamilton** Terracotta Multi Cream
35	Wallpaper **Jocelyn** Terracotta Multi Cream

TERRACOTTA & MOSS

TERRACOTTA

Jocelyn
F544 Terracotta Multi Cream   *342233*

Hamilton
F505 Terracotta Multi Cream   *092233*

Queen Anne's Needlework
F10 Terracotta/Oak/Cream   *070452*

Simla
F516 Multi Terracotta   *331398*

Maypole
F634 Terracotta Multi Cream   *385233*

Terracotta
020111

Light Terracotta *020294*

Dandelion
F335 Terracotta/Moss/Cream   *302270*

Milfoil
L570 Cream/Terracotta   *040030*

Petite Fleur
R150 Terracotta/Cream   *026029*

 WALLPAPER   VINYL WALL-COVERING    COUNTRY FURNISHING COTTON   DRAWING ROOM FABRIC   LINEN UNION   DOBBY   UPHOLSTERY FABRIC   CHINTZ

MOSS

Tulips
F488 Multi Stone   327397

Petra
F671 Moss   357102

Wild Clematis
S65 Moss/White   004024

Emperor
F210 Terracotta Multi Cream   145233

Wild Clematis
S65 White/Moss   004017

Moss
020102

Nutmeg
S49 Moss/White   015024
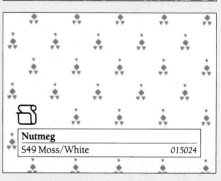

Wood Violet
F753 Terracotta/Moss/Cream   046270

Cricket Stripe
F369 Terracotta/Moss/Cream   185449
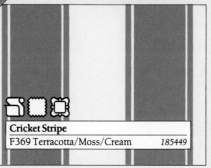

Imogen
F471 Cherry Multi White   097244
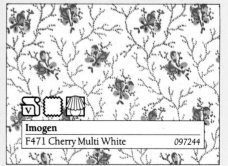

PLASTIC COATED FABRIC | GLOSS PAINT | FLAT PAINT | CERAMIC TILES | LAMP-SHADES | DINING COLLECTION | CUSHIONS | BEDLINEN

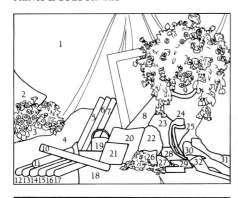

1	Drawing Room Fabric **Country Roses** Rose Multi White
2	Flat Bordered Cushion **Rose** with **Stratford** Border
3	Country Furn. Cotton **Rowan** Light Rose/Moss/White
4	Lattice Patchwork Quilt **Rose**
5	Vinyl Wallcovering **Campion** Rose/White
6	Vinyl Wallcovering **Rowan** Light Rose/Moss/White
7	Vinyl Wallcovering **Sweetbriar** Rose Multi White
8	Country Furnishing Cotton **Rosamund** Rose Multi White
9	Cord Tie-Back **Rose**
10	Vinyl Wallcovering **Wickerwork** Rose/White
11	Vinyl Wallcovering **Salon** Rose/Candy
12	Vinyl Wallcovering **Wood Violet** Rose/Moss/White
13	Vinyl Wallcovering **Cottage Sprig** Rose/Moss/White
14	Vinyl Wallcovering **Kate** Rose/Moss/White
15	Wallpaper **Clover** Rose/White
16	Vinyl Wallcovering **Campion** White/Rose
17	Vinyl Wallcovering **Candy Stripe** Rose/White
18	Drawing Room Fabric **Country Roses** Rose Multi White
19	Flat Paint **Soft Rose**
20	Tapestry Cushion Kit **Blue Ribbons** Smoke Multi Stone
21	Floor & Wall Tile **Rose**
22	Round Frilled Cushion **Kate** Rose/Moss/White
23	Square Piped Chintz Cushion **Rose**
24	Bias Binding **Rose**
25	Braid **Rose/Moss/White**
26	Tapestry Pin Cushion Kit **Kate** Rose/Moss/White
27	Plain Gimp **Rose**
28	Wall Tiles **Pavilion** Rose/White
29	Wall Tiles **Cottage Sprig** Rose/Moss/White
30	Wallpaper Border **Juliet** Rose Multi White
31	Wallpaper Border **Rosy Swag** Rose Multi White
32	Wallpaper Border **Trompe** Rose/White

ROSE

ROSE

Sweetbriar
F388 Rose Multi White   *179144*

Clover
F43 Rose/White   *075066*

Rose
020114

Soft Rose *020292*

Campion
R143 Rose/White   *021066*

Campion
R143 White/Rose   *021067*

Cottage Sprig
P767 Rose/Moss/White   *053080*

Bindweed
F36 Rose Multi White   *073144*

Palmetto
F303 Rose/Moss/White   *184080*

 WALLPAPER   VINYL WALL-COVERING   COUNTRY FURNISHING COTTON   DRAWING ROOM FABRIC   LINEN UNION   DOBBY   UPHOLSTERY FABRIC   CHINTZ

ROSE

Harebell
L631 Rose/Moss/White   *056080*

Kate
F373 Rose/Moss/White   *173080*

Mary Ann
F341 Rose/Sky Blue Multi White   *172477*

Wickerwork
L571 Rose/White   *141066*

Candy Stripe
G426 Rose/White   *039066*

Wickerwork
L571 White/Rose   *041067*

Wood Violet
P753 Rose/Moss/White   *046080*

 PLASTIC COATED FABRIC   GLOSS PAINT   FLAT PAINT   CERAMIC TILES   LAMP-SHADES   DINING COLLECTION   CUSHIONS   BEDLINEN

ROSE

Rosamund
F590 Rose Multi White   *094144*

Rowan
F686 Light Rose/Moss/White   *365533*

Country Roses
F430 Rose Multi White   *089144*

White
020100

Sugar Pink
020327

Garlands
F340 Rose Multi Stone   *177478*

Convolvulus
L610 Multi Rose   *060459*

Jaipur
F332 Multi Light Mulberry   *175253*

Poona
F328 Leaf Green/Raspberry/White   *176254*

Salon
F112 Rose/Candy   *129220*

 WALLPAPER   VINYL WALL-COVERING   COUNTRY FURNISHING COTTON   DRAWING ROOM FABRIC   LINEN UNION   DOBBY   UPHOLSTERY FABRIC   CHINTZ

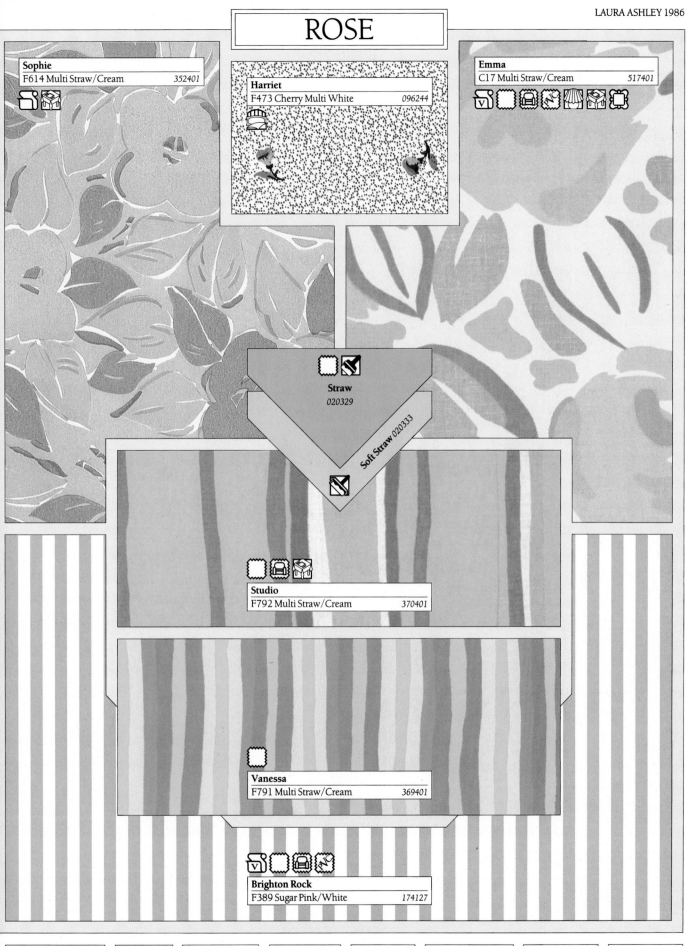

ROSE

Sophie
F614 Multi Straw/Cream   *352401*

Harriet
F473 Cherry Multi White   *096244*

Emma
C17 Multi Straw/Cream   *517401*

Straw
020329

Soft Straw *020333*

Studio
F792 Multi Straw/Cream   *370401*

Vanessa
F791 Multi Straw/Cream   *369401*

Brighton Rock
F389 Sugar Pink/White   *174127*

 PLASTIC COATED FABRIC	GLOSS PAINT	FLAT PAINT	CERAMIC TILES	LAMP-SHADES	DINING COLLECTION	CUSHIONS	BEDLINEN

1. Rnd. Frilled Cushion **Regency Stripe** Apricot/Aqua./Wh.

2. Country Furnishing Cotton **Salon** Apricot/Apricot Wash

3. Mosaic Patchwork Quilt **Apricot/Aquamarine**

4. Country Furnishing Cotton **Salon** Mint/Aquamarine

5. Country Furn. Cotton **Brighton Rock** Apricot/White

6. Wallpaper **Salon** Mint/Aquamarine

7. Wallpaper **Stipple** Apricot/Primrose

8. Vinyl Wallcovering **Palmetto** Apricot/Aqua./Apr. Wash

9. Sq. Frilled Cushion **Regency Stripe** Aqua./Apricot/White

10. Coolie Lampshades **Apricot & Aquamarine**

11. Small Lampshade **Salon** Apricot/Apricot Wash

12. Small Lampbase **Apricot**

13. Country Furnishing Cotton **Penelope** Mint Multi White

14. Wall Tiles **Pavilion** Aquamarine/White & Apricot/White

15	Flat Paint **Soft Apricot & Light Aquamarine**	22	Country Furnishing Cotton **Floribunda** Multi Apricot
16	Tapestry Cushion Kit **Kew Gardens** Mint Multi White	23	Country Furn. Cotton **Brighton Rock** Aquamarine/White
17	Vinyl Wallcovering **Regency Stripe** Apricot/Aqua./Wh.	24	Drawing Room Fabric **Clarissa** Apricot Multi White
18	Vinyl Wallcovering **Regency Stripe** Aqua./Apricot/Wh.	25	Country Furn. Cotton **Palmetto** Apricot/Aqua./Apr. Wash
19	Vinyl Wallcovering **Floribunda** Multi Apricot	26	Gimp **Apricot**
20	Country Furnishing Cotton **Emma** Multi Apricot/White	27	Wallpaper Border **Stratford** Aquamarine/Apricot/White
21	Country Furn. Cotton **Regency Stripe** Apricot/Aqua./Wh.	28	Country Furn. Cotton **Palmetto** Aqua./Apricot/White

AQUAMARINE & APRICOT

APRICOT

Floribunda
L577 Multi Apricot   042096

Emma
C17 Multi Apricot/White   517415

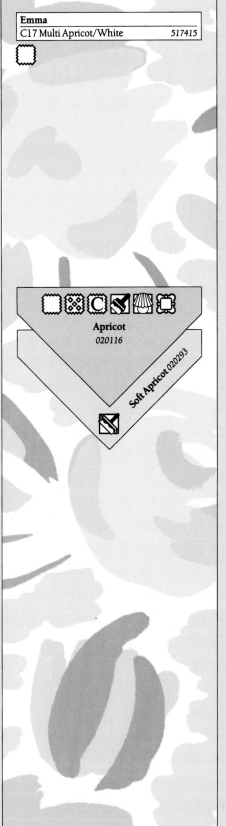

Apricot
020116

Soft Apricot *020293*

Stipple
F119 Apricot/Primrose   128241

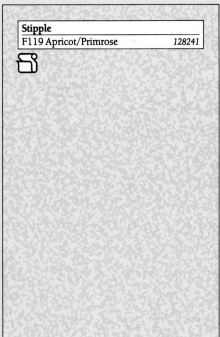

Palmetto
F303 Apricot/Aqua/Apricot Wash   184267

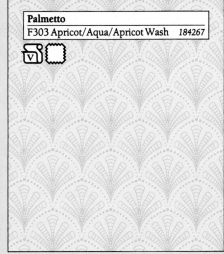

Salon
F112 Apricot/Apricot Wash   129266

Salon
F112 Mint/Aquamarine   129212

Palmetto
F303 Aquamarine/Apricot/White   184268

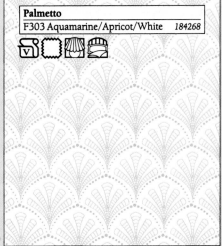

AQUAMARINE

Sweetbriar
F388 Apricot Multi White   *179146*

Penelope
F535 Mint Multi White   *095396*

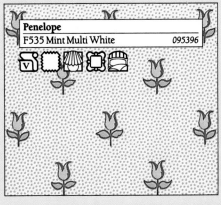

Clarissa
F45 Apricot Multi White   *076146*

Kew Gardens
F484 Mint Multi White   *090396*

Aquamarine
020340

Lt. Aquamarine *020290*

Regency Stripe
F374 Apricot/Aquamarine/White   *197265*

Regency Stripe
F374 Aquamarine/Apricot/White   *197268*

Brighton Rock
F389 Apricot/White   *174074*

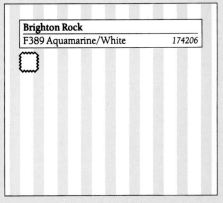

Brighton Rock
F389 Aquamarine/White   *174206*

 PLASTIC COATED FABRIC   GLOSS PAINT   FLAT PAINT   CERAMIC TILES   LAMP-SHADES    DINING COLLECTION   CUSHIONS   BEDLINEN

CUSTOMER INFORMATION

COLOUR MATCHING

Whilst every effort is made to ensure as close a match as possible, colours shown in Laura Ashley magazines may not be an exact reproduction of the original tones found in the products. It should also be noted that there may be slight variations in colour between each batch of fabric and wallpaper. There may also be variation between different types of product.

SIZES

All measurements quoted in this magazine are approximate, and may vary slightly in some cases. Inch equivalents are calculated to the nearest approximate measurement.

SHRINKAGE

Please allow 3-5% shrinkage on all fabrics.

DESIGN

Although every effort is made to supply each product as it is shown in the magazine, some variation in design may sometimes be necessary.

SAMPLES

To assist with your selection of Laura Ashley furnishings, up to six small samples of fabric or wallpaper can be supplied free of charge — by request to the Mail Order Customer Services address on the right. These samples are for guidance only and there may be a slight difference in colour tone due to batch variances.

FEATURED PRODUCTS

As far as possible, Laura Ashley products are used in the room sets and other photographs in this magazine. However, from time to time other products may have to be used to create a particular effect.

INSTRUCTIONS FOR USE

May we draw attention to the importance of reading and following the instructions given on the care and use of Laura Ashley products in order to ensure full performance of, and satisfaction with, the merchandise.

DISCONTINUATIONS

The collection outlined in this magazine is intended to be available until December 1986. From 1st November 1986 Laura Ashley shop staff and the Customer Services Departments at the addresses on the right will be in a position to advise you of any references which are unlikely to be carried in the 1987 range of Home Furnishings.

STOCKING

As our shops are limited in space, some may not carry the full range in stock at any one time. However, all Laura Ashley furnishing shops are normally able to take your personal order for any of the items in the collection.

PRICES

Whilst every effort is made to maintain the prices given in this magazine, unavoidable adjustments may occasionally take place. Shop staff and Customer Services Departments will be pleased to advise you in the case of alterations.

SALES TAXES

We must collect tax for merchandise delivered to areas where we have shops.

ADVANCE INFORMATION AND MAIL ORDER

If you would like to receive advance information on our future collections and magazines, or require further information about our Mail Order Service, please contact: Mail Order Customer Services, address below. If you have any queries concerning products please contact:
Mail Order Customer Services, Laura Ashley Inc, 1300 MacArthur Boulevard, Mahwah, New Jersey, N. J. 07430,
Tel 1 800 367 2000 Monday - Friday 8am - 5pm.

REFUNDS AND COMPLAINTS

We hope you will be fully satisfied with your purchases. However, should you have any cause for dissatisfaction, please, if possible, take the article in question, together with the receipt, to the original shop of purchase or contact Customer Services. We regret that refunds cannot be made outside the country of original purchase.
If you are at all dissatisfied with any service which you have received, please contact:
The Customer Services Manager,
Laura Ashley Inc, 1300 MacArthur Boulevard, Mahwah, New Jersey, N.J. 07430,
Tel 1 800 367 2000.

FABRIC REPEAT SIZES (to nearest cm or ½in). Stripes & plains have no repeats. Please note: recommended wallpaper repeat is 64 cm (25 ins) for all designs.

In order to match certain prints when joining two pieces of the same fabric, it may be necessary to lose a certain amount of fabric. For further information on this please contact Customer Services at the address above.

	cm	ins		cm	ins		cm	ins		cm	ins		cm	ins
Albert	8	3	Damask	64	25	Harebell	21	8	Mr. Jones	5	2	Sara Jane	8	3
Attic	3	1	Dandelion	16	6	Imogen	4	1½	Nutmeg	3	1	Scottish Thistle	3	1
Bembridge	9	2½	Edward	8	3	Indienne	21	8	Oak Leaves	2.5	1	Sea Spray	2	1
Bindweed	8	3	Emma	32	12½	Jaipur	13	5	Oriana	2	1	Shepherd's Purse	22	8½
Campion	22	8½	Emmeline	64	25	Joy	64	25	Paisley	2	1	Simla	3	1
Carousel	21.5	8½	Emperor	64	25	Kate	4	1½	Palmetto	2	1	Stitchwort	1	½
Cherries	5	2	English Garden	32	12½	Kew Gardens	64	25	Penelope	4	1½	Summertime	32	12½
Chinoiserie	21	8½	Favorita	64	25	Lily of the Valley	21	8	Petite Fleur	8	3	Trefoil	4	1½
Clarissa	32	12½	Florentina	16	6	Malcolm	21	8	Petra	21	8	Tulips	21	8
Clover	4	1½	Floribunda	17	6½	Mary Ann	11	4	Polly	2	1	Venetia	64	25
Convolvulus	19	7½	Fretwork	5	2	Maypole	32	12½	Poona	4	1½	White Bower	64	25
Cordelia	32	12½	Garlands	64	25	Meadow Flowers	30	12	Q.Anne's Needlework	3	1	Wickerwork	3	1
Cornflowers	4	1½	Grand Paisley	32	13	Michaelmas	16	6	Rectory Garden	5	2	Wild Clematis	9	3½
Cottage Sprig	10	4	Grapes	11	4	Milfoil	8	3	Rosamund	8	3	Wind Spray	22	8½
Country Roses	64	25	Hamilton	32	12½	Ming	13	5	Rowan	4	1½	Wood Violet	7	2½
Crystal	21	8½	Harbour	3	1	Morning Parlour	16	6	Salon	16	6			

WALLPAPER CALCULATOR (No. of rolls needed for walls)

Wall height from skirting in feet	Measurement round room in feet (inc. doors and windows):												
	33	36	39	43	46	49	52	56	59	62	66	69	72
6'6" to 7'2"	5	5	5	6	6	7	7	7	8	8	9	9	10
7'2" to 7'10"	5	5	6	6	7	7	8	8	9	9	10	10	10
7'10" to 8'6"	5	6	6	7	7	8	8	9	9	10	10	11	11
8'6" to 9'2"	6	6	7	7	8	9	9	10	11	11	12	12	12
9'2" to 9'10"	6	7	7	8	8	9	10	11	11	12	12	13	13
9'10" to 10'6"	6	7	8	8	9	10	10	11	11	12	13	13	14
10'6" to 11'2"	7	7	8	9	9	10	11	11	12	13	13	14	15

METRIC WALLPAPER CALCULATOR (No. of rolls needed for walls)

Wall height from skirting in metres	Measurement round room in metres (inc. doors and windows):												
	10	11	12	13	14	15	16	17	18	19	20	21	22
2.0 to 2.2	5	5	5	6	6	7	7	7	8	8	9	9	10
2.2 to 2.4	5	5	6	6	7	7	8	8	9	9	10	10	10
2.4 to 2.6	5	6	6	7	7	8	8	9	9	10	10	11	11
2.6 to 2.8	6	6	7	7	8	9	9	10	11	11	12	12	12
2.8 to 3.0	6	7	7	8	8	9	10	11	11	12	12	13	13
3.0 to 3.2	6	7	8	8	9	10	10	11	11	12	13	13	14
3.2 to 3.4	7	7	8	9	9	10	11	11	12	13	13	14	15

HOW TO ORDER

GENERAL INFORMATION

1. To order you can call toll free 1-800-367-2000, 24 hours a day, seven days a week. Or you can complete the attached order form and mail to Laura Ashley Inc., Mail Order Department, 1300 MacArthur Boulevard, Mahwah, New Jersey 07430. Please fill in the form as shown in the example.

2. Minimum fabric length supplied is one yard. Please order full yard lengths only. The maximum continuous lengths in which fabric can be supplied are: Country Furnishing Cotton 35 yards, Chintz 25 yards, Upholstery Fabric 25 yards, Drawing Room Fabric 35 yards, Fabric Borders 20 yards, Plastic Coated Fabric 25 yards, Lining Fabric 50 yards.

3. We normally dispatch all goods within 72 hours, but please allow up to 14 days for delivery. We will inform you if, for any reason, we cannot send your order within this time. For information regarding your order we may be contacted at the number and address noted above. With any customer service problems, please note the name of the Laura Ashley Representative.

4. We want you to be fully satisfied with your purchase. If any of our products do not meet your expectations, at any time, please return them, post paid and in good condition, and we will refund your original cost. We would be grateful if you could quote your order number upon return. However, we regret that refunds can only be made on Made to Measure Curtains and cut fabric if they are faulty or do not comply with your original order.

5. We aim to maintain prices throughout the year but reserve the right to change them without notice. We will inform you of price changes before shipping your order.

ORDER FORM

1. *Product Code* – located in description of product.
2. *Reference number* located in description of pattern/color.
3. *Description* – When describing curtains or furniture, please include material pattern and type of curtain or furniture.
4. *Colourway* – Color description found next to product (i.e., smoke/cream).
5. *Number of Pairs or Blinds* – The number of curtain pairs or blinds to be made. For curtain panel indicate this as ½.
6. *Type of material* – Indicate type of material from list below:
   Upholstery
   Dobby
   Country Furnishing Cotton (CFC)
   Chintz
   Drawing Room Fabric (DRF)
   Linen Union
7. *Length* –
   A. For Curtains: Measure the length of curtain needed from the point where you require the top of the curtain heading to be, to the point to which you require the curtain to hang. (Please note that the lengths quoted are for pricing purposes only, the curtains will be finished to the specific lengths given). For intermediate lengths, select the price of the next group up.
   B. For Blinds: Measure the length from the point where the top of the blind heading is to be to the point

at which the bottom of the blind is required when fully lowered. Festoon blinds are made slightly longer than the given length to allow for the festoon effect. For intermediate lengths select the price of the blind the next size up.

8. *Width* –
   A. For Curtains: Measure the width of your curtain rail (taking care to note that this may not be the same as the width of your window). Consult the table below matching the length of the rail to the width size.

Rail Widths: ins Up To cm	41 105	61 155	81 205	100 255	121 302
Double Fullness: wdth Pair of Curtains cm	43" 109	64" 163	89" 226	110" 279	131" 333

   B. For Blinds: Measure the final width of the blind rail you require, whether the blind is to be fitted inside or outside a recess. If it is to go outside a recess, an overlap of at least 9.5 cm (3¾ ins) each side recommended. Please insure that measurements are accurate.

9. *Cleaning instructions* – We recommend dry cleaning for all curtains and blinds. Washing is possible but the unavoidable variation in the washing performance of the curtain, blind and lining fabrics may result in some differential shrinkage.
10. *Delivery* – As all items are individually finished by hand, six weeks is the usual time to allow for Curtains & Blinds.
11. *Unit Price* – Price for an object (Please see next page for Curtain & Blind prices).
12. *Quantity* – Number of objects ordered.
13. *Merchandise Total* – Quantity ordered multiplied by unit price.

DRAWING ROOM CURTAINS

All prices are per pair. Finished Length up to: In.	Cm.	WIDTH OF PLAIN CURTAIN 41 / 105	61 / 155	81 / 205	100 / 255	120 / 305	140 / 355	159 / 405	FRILLS ADD
48	122	$113	$168	$224	$280	$336	$390	$445	$9
54	137	$125	$187	$249	$311	$373	$433	$487	$10
60	152	$136	$206	$274	$342	$410	$477	$536	$11
66	168	$151	$224	$300	$375	$450	$523	$590	$12
72	183	$163	$244	$325	$407	$487	$567	$639	$13
78	198	$176	$263	$350	$438	$525	$611	$689	$14
84	213	$188	$282	$375	$469	$562	$654	$739	$16
90	229	$202	$302	$401	$502	$602	$698	$792	$17
96	244	$214	$320	$426	$533	$639	$744	$842	$18
102	259	$226	$339	$451	$564	$677	$788	$892	$19
108	274	$239	$358	$476	$596	$714	$832	$942	$20
114	290	$252	$378	$503	$629	$754	$878	$995	$21
120	305	$265	$396	$528	$660	$792	$922	$1045	$22
126	320	$277	$415	$553	$691	$829	$965	$1095	$23
132	335	$290	$434	$578	$722	$866	$1009	$1144	$24
138	350	$303	$454	$604	$756	$906	$1055	$1198	$26
144	366	$316	$473	$629	$787	$944	$1099	$1247	$27
150	381	$328	$491	$654	$818	$981	$1143	$1297	$28
156	396	$341	$510	$679	$849	$1018	$1186	$1347	$29
162	411	$353	$529	$704	$880	$1056	$1230	$1397	$30
168	427	$366	$548	$731	$913	$1096	$1276	$1450	$31

COUNTRY FURNISHING COTTON CURTAINS

All prices are per pair. Finished Length up to: In.	Cm.	WIDTH OF PLAIN CURTAIN 41 / 105	61 / 155	81 / 205	100 / 255	120 / 305	140 / 355	159 / 405	FRILLS ADD
48	122	$91	$136	$181	$226	$271	$315	$368	$7
54	137	$101	$151	$201	$252	$302	$350	$392	$8
60	152	$110	$166	$221	$277	$332	$386	$432	$8
66	168	$122	$181	$243	$304	$364	$423	$475	$10
72	183	$132	$198	$263	$329	$394	$458	$515	$10
78	198	$142	$213	$283	$354	$424	$494	$556	$11
84	213	$152	$228	$303	$379	$455	$529	$596	$11
90	229	$163	$244	$325	$406	$487	$564	$639	$12
96	244	$173	$259	$345	$432	$517	$602	$679	$13
102	259	$183	$274	$365	$457	$548	$637	$720	$14
108	274	$193	$289	$385	$482	$578	$673	$760	$14
114	290	$204	$306	$407	$509	$610	$710	$803	$15
120	305	$214	$321	$427	$534	$640	$746	$843	$16
126	320	$224	$336	$447	$559	$671	$781	$884	$17
132	335	$234	$351	$467	$585	$701	$816	$924	$18
138	350	$245	$367	$489	$611	$733	$854	$967	$19
144	366	$255	$382	$509	$637	$763	$889	$1007	$20
150	381	$265	$397	$529	$662	$794	$924	$1048	$20
156	396	$276	$412	$549	$687	$824	$960	$1088	$21
162	411	$286	$428	$570	$712	$854	$995	$1128	$23
168	427	$296	$444	$591	$739	$886	$1032	$1171	$24

COUNTRY FURNISHING COTTON ROMAN BLINDS

Finished Length up to: In.	Cm.	WIDTH OF BLIND 21 / 54	42 / 108	59 / 150
42	107	$127	$160	$217
54	137	$147	$186	$254
66	168	$165	$210	$290
78	198	$184	$233	$326
90	229	$203	$258	$363
102	259	$221	$282	$398
114	290	$240	$306	$434
126	320	$259	$331	$471

DRAWING ROOM FABRIC ROMAN BLINDS

In.	Cm.	21 / 54	42 / 108	59 / 150
42	107	$142	$179	$250
54	137	$165	$209	$295
66	168	$188	$238	$340
78	198	$210	$267	$384
90	229	$233	$297	$429
102	259	$255	$326	$473
114	290	$277	$355	$518
126	320	$300	$385	$563

CHINTZ ROMAN BLINDS

In.	Cm.	21 / 54	42 / 108	59 / 150
42	107	$132	$163	$222
54	137	$150	$188	$260
66	168	$169	$213	$298
78	198	$188	$237	$334
90	229	$208	$263	$372
102	259	$226	$287	$409
114	290	$246	$312	$446

CHINTZ CURTAINS

All prices are per pair. Finished Length up to: In.	Cm.	WIDTH OF PLAIN CURTAIN 41 / 105	61 / 155	81 / 205	100 / 255	120 / 305	140 / 355	159 / 405	FRILLS ADD
48	122	$96	$144	$191	$239	$287	$333	$380	$7
54	137	$107	$160	$212	$266	$319	$370	$414	$8
60	152	$116	$176	$234	$292	$350	$407	$457	$9
66	168	$129	$192	$256	$321	$384	$447	$502	$10
72	183	$139	$208	$278	$347	$416	$484	$545	$11
78	198	$150	$225	$299	$374	$448	$521	$587	$12
84	213	$161	$240	$320	$401	$480	$559	$630	$13
90	229	$172	$258	$343	$429	$514	$596	$675	$14
96	244	$183	$273	$364	$456	$546	$636	$718	$15
102	259	$194	$289	$385	$482	$578	$673	$760	$15
108	274	$204	$305	$407	$509	$610	$710	$803	$16
114	290	$216	$322	$429	$537	$644	$750	$848	$17
120	305	$226	$338	$451	$564	$676	$787	$891	$18
126	320	$237	$354	$472	$590	$708	$824	$933	$19
132	335	$248	$370	$493	$617	$740	$862	$976	$20
138	350	$259	$387	$516	$645	$774	$901	$1021	$21
144	366	$270	$403	$537	$672	$806	$938	$1064	$22
150	381	$280	$419	$559	$699	$838	$976	$1106	$23
156	396	$291	$435	$580	$725	$870	$1013	$1149	$24
162	411	$302	$451	$601	$752	$902	$1058	$1192	$24
168	427	$313	$468	$624	$780	$936	$1090	$1237	$25

Coordinating tie-backs are available to enhance the look of your made-to-measure curtains. Please see page 81 for details.

CHINTZ FESTOON BLINDS

Finished Length up to: In.	Cm.	WIDTH OF BLIND					
		28 / 70	38 / 98	46 / 118	52 / 131	64 / 164	70 / 179
36	91	$134	$147	$157	$208	$220	$230
42	107	$146	$158	$169	$225	$238	$248
48	122	$157	$170	$181	$243	$256	$266
54	137	$168	$181	$192	$261	$275	$285
60	152	$180	$193	$204	$279	$293	$303
66	168	$191	$204	$216	$297	$311	$321
72	183	$203	$216	$227	$315	$329	$339
78	198	$214	$228	$239	$332	$347	$357
84	213	$226	$239	$251	$350	$365	$376
90	229	$237	$251	$262	$368	$383	$394
96	244	$248	$263	$274	$386	$401	$412
102	259	$259	$274	$286	$404	$419	$438
108	274	$271	$285	$297	$422	$437	$448
114	290	$282	$297	$309	$448	$455	$466
120	305	$294	$309	$321	$457	$473	$484

LARGER SIZES AVAILABLE. PRICES UPON REQUEST. 1-800-367-2000.

COUNTRY FURNISHING COTTON FESTOON BLINDS

Finished Length up to: In.	Cm.	WIDTH OF BLIND					
		28 / 70	38 / 98	46 / 118	52 / 131	64 / 164	70 / 179
36	91	$130	$143	$153	$201	$214	$224
42	107	$141	$153	$164	$218	$231	$241
48	122	$152	$164	$175	$235	$248	$258
54	137	$162	$175	$186	$252	$265	$275
60	152	$173	$186	$197	$269	$282	$292
66	168	$184	$197	$208	$286	$300	$310
72	183	$195	$208	$219	$302	$316	$327
78	198	$205	$219	$230	$319	$334	$344
84	213	$216	$230	$241	$336	$351	$361
90	229	$227	$241	$252	$353	$368	$378
96	244	$237	$252	$263	$370	$385	$396
102	259	$248	$262	$274	$387	$402	$413
108	274	$259	$273	$285	$404	$419	$430
114	298	$270	$284	$296	$421	$436	$447
120	305	$280	$295	$308	$437	$453	$464

LARGER SIZES AVAILABLE. PRICES UPON REQUEST. 1-800-367-2000.

DRAWING ROOM FABRIC FESTOON BLINDS

Finished Length up to: In.	Cm.	WIDTH OF BLIND					
		28 / 70	38 / 98	46 / 118	52 / 131	64 / 164	70 / 179
36	91	$148	$161	$172	$228	$241	$251
42	107	$161	$174	$185	$249	$263	$273
48	122	$175	$188	$199	$270	$284	$294
54	137	$188	$202	$213	$291	$305	$316
60	152	$202	$215	$227	$312	$326	$337
66	168	$215	$229	$241	$333	$348	$358
72	183	$228	$243	$255	$354	$369	$380
78	198	$242	$256	$268	$375	$390	$401
84	213	$255	$258	$282	$396	$412	$423
90	229	$268	$284	$296	$417	$433	$444
96	244	$282	$297	$310	$438	$454	$465
102	259	$295	$311	$324	$458	$475	$487
108	274	$309	$325	$338	$480	$497	$508
114	290	$322	$338	$352	$500	$518	$530
120	305	$335	$352	$366	$521	$539	$551

LARGER SIZES AVAILABLE. PRICES UPON REQUEST. 1-800-367-2000.

COUNTRY FURNISHING COTTON VALANCE

Finished Length up to: In.	Cm.	WIDTH OF VALANCE						
		41 / 105	61 / 155	81 / 205	100 / 255	120 / 305	140 / 355	159 / 405
15	38	$46	$66	$91	$111	$118	$137	$162
18	46	$54	$77	$106	$127	$136	$159	$188
21	53	$61	$88	$120	$148	$154	$181	$213
24	61	$68	$99	$135	$166	$173	$203	$239
27	68	$77	$110	$150	$184	$191	$225	$265

DRAWING ROOM VALANCE

Finished Length up to: In.	Cm.	WIDTH OF VALANCE						
		41 / 105	61 / 155	81 / 205	100 / 255	120 / 305	140 / 355	159 / 405
15	38	$62	$89	$124	$150	$159	$186	$220
18	46	$72	$104	$142	$172	$183	$214	$253
21	53	$82	$118	$161	$197	$207	$243	$286
24	61	$92	$132	$177	$221	$231	$271	$320
27	68	$102	$146	$199	$245	$255	$300	$353

CHINTZ VALANCE

Finished Length up to: In.	Cm.	WIDTH OF VALANCE						
		41 / 105	61 / 155	81 / 205	100 / 255	120 / 305	140 / 355	159 / 405
15	38	$54	$76	$106	$128	$136	$158	$188
18	46	$62	$89	$122	$147	$157	$183	$216
21	53	$70	$101	$138	$170	$177	$208	$245
24	61	$78	$114	$155	$190	$198	$233	$274
27	68	$88	$126	$171	$211	$219	$258	$303

If you need any assistance in determining your needs for made-to-measure curtains, blinds, or valances, please call our toll-free number 1-800-367-2000. Our customer service representatives will be happy to help you.

CALIFORNIA

Corte Madera The Village at Corte Madera, Corte Madera 94925	(415) 924-5770
Costa Mesa South Coast Plaza, Costa Mesa 92626	(714) 545-9322
La Jolla 7852 Girard Avenue, La Jolla 92037	(619) 459-3733
Beverly Center 121 N. La Cienega Blvd., Los Angeles 90048	(213) 854-0490
Palm Springs Desert Fashion Plaza, Palm Springs 92262*	
Palo Alto Stanford Shopping Center, Palo Alto 94304	(415) 328-0560
Bullocks Pasadena 401 S. Lake Avenue, Pasadena 91101	(818) 792-0211 ext. 265
Redondo Beach The Galleria at South Bay, Redondo Beach 90278	(213) 542-4436
San Diego 247 Horton Plaza, San Diego 92101	(619) 234-0663
San Francisco I 1827 Union Street, San Francsico 94123	(415) 922-7200
San Francisco II 563 Sutter Street, San Francisco 94102	(415) 788-0190
Santa Barbara La Cumbre Galleria, Santa Barbara 93110	(805) 682-8878
Walnut Creek Broadway Shopping Center, Walnut Creek 94596	(415) 947-5920
Bullocks Westwood 10861 Weyburn Ave., Westwood 90024	(213) 208-4211 ext. 284

COLORADO

Denver 1439 Larimer Street, Denver 80202	(303) 571-0050

CONNECTICUT

Hartford West Farms Mall, Farmington 06032	(203) 521-8967
Stamford Stamford Town Center, Stamford 06902	(203) 324-1067
Westport 85 Main Street, Westport 06880	(203) 226-7495

FLORIDA

Boca Raton Town Center at Boca Raton, Boca Raton 33431	(305) 368-5622
Fort Lauderdale Galleria at Fort Lauderdale, Ft. Laud. 33304	(305) 563-2300
Miami The Falls, Miami 33176*	
Palm Beach 320 Worth Avenue, Palm Beach 33480	(305) 832-3188
Tampa Old Hyde Park Village, Tampa 33606*	

GEORGIA

Atlanta I Lenox Square, Atlanta 30326	(404) 231-0685
Atlanta II Perimeter Mall, Atlanta 30346	(404) 395-6027

HAWAII

Honolulu Ala Moana Center, Honolulu 96814	(808) 942-5200

ILLINOIS

Chicago Watertower Place, Chicago 60611	(312) 951-8004
Northbrook Northbrook Court, Northbrook 60062	(312) 480-1660
Oakbrook Oakbrook Center, Oakbrook 60521	(312) 789-9195
Woodfield Woodfield Mall, Schaumburg 60195	(312) 519-9110

INDIANA

Indianapolis Fashion Mall, Indianapolis 46240	(317) 848-9855

KENTUCKY

Louisville Louisville Galleria, Louisville 40202†	

LOUISIANA

New Orleans Canal Place, New Orleans 70130	(504) 522-9403

MARYLAND

Annapolis 139 Main Street, Annapolis 21401	(301) 268-6906
Baltimore Harborplace, Pratt Street Pavilion, Baltimore 21202	(301) 539-0500
White Flint White Flint Mall, Kensington 20895	(301) 984-3223

MASSACHUSETTS

Boston 83 Newbury Street, Boston 02116	(617) 536-0505
Cambridge Charles Square, Cambridge 02138	(617) 576-3690
Chestnut Hill The Mall at Chestnut Hill, Chestnut Hill 02167	(617) 965-7640

MICHIGAN

Detroit Twelve Oaks Mall, Novi 48050	(313) 348-9260
Troy Somerset Mall, Troy 48084	(313) 649-0890

MINNESOTA

Minneapolis City Center, Minneapolis 55402	(612) 332-6066

MISSOURI

Kansas City Country Club Plaza, Kansas City 64112	(816) 931-0731
St. Louis I Plaza Frontenac, St. Louis 63131	(314) 993-4410
St. Louis II St. Louis Centre, St. Louis 63101	(314) 421-4931

NEW JERSEY

Hackensack Riverside Square, Hackensack 07601	(201) 488-0130
Paramus Paramus Park, Paramus 07652	(201) 599-0650
Princeton Palmer Square, Princeton 08542	(609) 683-4760
Short Hills The Mall at Short Hills, Short Hills 07078	(201) 467-5657

NEW YORK

Manhasset Americana Shopping Center, Manhasset 11030	(516) 365-4636
New York City 714 Madison Ave., 10021 (home furnishings only)	(212) 735-5000
New York City 398 Columbus Ave., 10024	(212) 496-5151
New York City 21 East 57th Street, 10022 (fashion only)	(212) 735-1010
New York City South Street Seaport, 10038	(212) 809-3555
Vernon Hills 696 White Plains Rd., Eastchester, 10583	(914) 723-8500

OHIO

Beachwood Beachwood Place, Beachwood 44122	(216) 831-7621

OKLAHOMA

Tulsa Utica Square, Tulsa 74114	(918) 749-5001

OREGON

Portland 622 S.W. Fifth Ave., Portland 97204†	

PENNSYLVANIA

Ardmore Suburban Square, Ardmore 19003	(215) 896-0208
Philadelphia 1721 Walnut Street, Philadelphia 19103	(215) 496-0492
Pittsburgh Station Square, Pittsburgh 15219	(412) 391-7993

RHODE ISLAND

Providence Davol Square Mall, Providence 02903	(401) 273-1120

TENNESSEE

Nashville The Mall at Green Hills, Nashville 37215	(615) 383-0131

TEXAS

Austin Highland Mall, Austin 78752	(512) 451-4036
Dallas I Galleria, Dallas 75240	(214) 980-9858
Dallas II North Park Center, Dallas 75225	(214) 369-5755
Fort Worth Hulen Mall, Fort Worth 76132	(817) 346-4666
Houston Galleria, Houston 77056	(713) 871-9669
Houston II West Oaks Mall, Houston 77082	(713) 558-6113
San Antonio North Star Mall, San Antonio 70216	(512) 377-2833

VERMONT

Burlington 23 Church Street, Burlington 05401	(802) 658-5006

VIRGINIA

Fair Oaks Fair Oaks Mall, Fairfax 22033	(703) 352-7960
Richmond Commercial Block, Richmond 23219	(804) 644-1050
Williamsburg Merchants Square, Williamsburg 23185	(804) 229-0353

WASHINGTON

Seattle 405 University Street, Seattle 98101	(206) 343-9637

WASHINGTON D.C.

Washington DC 3213 M St., N.W., Georgetown 20007	(202) 338-5481

CANADA

Montreal 2110 Crescent St., Montreal, Quebec H3G 2B8	(514) 284-9225
Toronto 18 Hazelton Ave., Toronto, Ontario M5R 2E2	(416) 922-7761
Vancouver 1171 Robson St., Vancouver, BC V6E 1B1	(604) 688-8729
Ottawa 136 Bank Street, Ottawa K1P 5N8	(613) 238-4882
Quebec Centre D'Achat Pl. Ste-Foy, 2452 Blvd., Wilfred Laurier Ste-Foy	(415) 659-6600
Bayview Bayview Village Shopping Center, Willowdale, Ontario M2K 1E6	(416) 223-9507

† Shops soon to be opened. For exact opening date, call toll free 1-800-367-2000.

* Shops recently opened.

FOR FASTEST ORDERING,

CALL 24 HOURS A DAY:

1-800-367-2000.

HF86-2

Send your order with payment to:
Laura Ashley Inc., P.O. Box 891, Mahwah, N.J. 07430--9990   or call toll free 1-800-367-2000.

My address and phone is	Delivery address if different from that on left
Mr/Mrs/Miss	Mr/Mrs/Miss
Address	Address

City	State	Zip	City	State	Zip
Phone			Phone		

Product Code No.	Reference Number	Product Description/ Pattern Name	Colourway	Unit Price	Quantity	Total Price
301	137013	INFINITY WALLPAPER	SMOKE	17.50	3 ROLLS	52.50

Made to Measure Curtains & Blinds Order Form (see how to order page for instructions and pages 172 & 173 for prices).

Fabric:										
Pattern	Type	Colourway	Reference Number	Length	Width	Unit Price	Number Pairs of Curtains	Number of Blinds	Frills Price if Applicable	Total Price
CORN-FLOWER	CFC	SAPPHIRE	187485	48	43	109	2		/	218

Furniture

Product Description	Product Code	Fabric:				Unit Price	Quantity	Total Price
		Pattern	Type	Colourway	Reference No.			
CARLISLE SOFA	7021	PETITE FLOWER	CFC	CREAM/SMOKE	026014	1,840	1	1,840

Shipping Charges:	If your zip code begins with: 010-229 you pay $5.00.	Total
(There is only one price per order)	300-499 you pay $5.50.	Add Local Tax
	500-994 you pay $6.00.	Add Shipping

I'll pay by Check/Money Order ☐ $ Visa ☐   Master Card ☐   American Express ☐   GRAND TOTAL

My Card Number is ☐☐☐☐ ☐☐☐ ☐☐☐ ☐☐☐ ☐☐☐   Exp. Date   Signed

Make check payable to "Laura Ashley Inc."

HF86-2

Send your order with payment to:
Laura Ashley Inc., P.O. Box 891, Mahwah, N.J. 07430-9990   or call toll free 1-800-367-2000.

My address and phone is	Delivery address if different from that on left
Mr/Mrs/Miss	Mr/Mrs/Miss
Address	Address

City	State	Zip	City	State	Zip
Phone			Phone		

Product Code No.	Reference Number	Product Description/ Pattern Name	Colourway	Unit Price	Quantity	Total Price

Made to Measure Curtains & Blinds Order Form (see how to order page for instructions and pages 172 & 173 for prices).

Fabric:

Pattern	Type	Colourway	Reference Number	Length	Width	Unit Price	Number Pairs of Curtains	Number of Blinds	Frills Price if Applicable	Total Price

Furniture

Product Description	Product Code	Fabric:				Unit Price	Quantity	Total Price
		Pattern	Type	Colourway	Reference No.			

Shipping Charges:　　　　If your zip code begins with: 010-229 you pay $5.00.　　　　Total

(There is only one price per order)　　　　300-499 you pay $5.50.　　　Add Local Tax

　　　　500-994 you pay $6.00.　　　Add Shipping

I'll pay by Check/Money Order ☐　$　　　Visa ☐　　Master Card ☐　　American Express ☐　　**GRAND TOTAL**

My Card Number is ☐☐☐☐ ☐☐☐ ☐☐☐ ☐☐☐ ☐☐☐　　Exp. Date　　　Signed

Make check payable to "Laura Ashley Inc."

Dear Customer,

Thank you for purchasing this latest annual edition of our Home Furnishings catalog.

We hope that you will find exactly the right items and ideas to help you complete your decorating.

For the first time this August, we will be publishing a supplemental edition to the annual catalog, bringing you more products and ideas for autumn decorating.

We will reserve a copy of this supplemental catalog in your name and be sure it is mailed to you as soon as it's off the press. Simply fill out your name and address on this order form and return it to us.

1st FOLD

3rd FOLD

2nd FOLD

3rd FOLD

NO POSTAGE
NECESSARY
IF MAILED
IN THE
UNITED STATES

BUSINESS REPLY MAIL
FIRST CLASS   PERMIT NO. 332   MAHWAH, NJ

Postage will be paid by addressee:

LAURA ASHLEY INC.
PO BOX 891
MAHWAH, NJ 07430-9990

FOR FASTEST ORDERING,
CALL 24 HOURS A DAY:
1-800-367-2000.